FAITHFUL CITY, FICKLE FOOTBALL

Chris Bishop

FAITHFUL CITY, FICKLE FOOTBALL

Resurrecting Worcester City,
the Sleeping Giant-Killers of Liverpool

pitch

First published by Pitch Publishing, 2025

1

(pitch)

Pitch Publishing
9 Donnington Park,
85 Birdham Road,
Chichester, West Sussex,
PO20 7AJ
www.pitchpublishing.co.uk
info@pitchpublishing.co.uk

A CIP catalogue record is available for this book
from the British Library.

ISBN 978 18015 095 4 1

Typesetting and origination by Pitch Publishing

MIX
Paper | Supporting
responsible forestry
FSC
www.fsc.org   FSC® C013604

Printed and bound in the UK on FSC® certified paper in line
with our continuing commitment to ethical business practices,
sustainability and the environment.

Printed and bound by CPI Antony Rowe, UK

Contents

Foreword

I HAVE worked in football for 52 years. I played for Everton in the UEFA Cup and 69 times for Derby County, yet Worcester City is my club. Always has been, always will be.

I played 145 times for Worcester City and scored seven goals. I was proud to manage my club for six years.

My first trip to St George's Lane came in the late 1960s. My family lived in Great Barr, Birmingham, but we had relatives in Worcester, who lived near the ground. It was a big trip for us before the M5 was built.

On one visit, Worcester City were playing at home; so, we went.

I shall never forget that first game under those bright lights which always seemed to shine magic into the night sky. There were nearly 4,000 people at St George's Lane, and you could feel the passion of the supporters from every corner of the ground.

On the night, crowd favourite George Bassett, a winger-turned-defender who scored 25 goals in 467 appearances, bossed the game; his speed and courage left an indelible impression. The crowds loved him because he was prepared to chase lost causes all night.

I remember thinking, 'If only I could play one day for Worcester City at St George's Lane.'

Little did I know that by 1976 I would be following in Bassett's talented footsteps.

Worcester City was the platform from which I launched my career in football. It was a special place where a tight-knit group of talented footballers trained hard and played for the love of the game.

To give you an idea of how much those players loved playing at St George's Lane, here is a story from the late 1970s.

Goalkeeper John Taylor, defender Billy Tetley, midfielder Graham Allner, midfielder Lionel Martin and I used to park in a pub car park in Birmingham and share a lift to Worcester in the battered old Austin Allegro belonging to Martin.

On the way into the city, around about Fernhill Heath, we would see carloads of farmers and fans from all over Worcestershire driving to the game.

From a few miles out you could see the floodlights of St George's Lane blazing from the city like beacons.

Long before we saw the lights, we would be on at Lionel, asking him if he could get his Allegro to go any faster. We were always excited to go to St George's Lane, we couldn't wait to get there; it was somewhere special to us.

That is why I was sad to hear of the decline and troubles of Worcester City in the last few years.

That is why I am pleased to hear of the club's renaissance under pragmatic new leadership. New owner Simon Lancaster is Worcester born-and-bred and appears to have a solid plan for a new ground as part of a brighter future for the club.

Worcestershire has long been a hotbed of football. Games between Worcester City, Stourbridge and Kidderminster Harriers have drawn large crowds for more than 120 years.

I am proud to have played for all three clubs and believe this is an important story to be told.

Allner also played for all three clubs and showed the strength of the high standards of this Worcestershire hotbed. He played for me at Worcester City in my day and learned a lot about running successful football teams from our manager Nobby Clark, reckoned by many to be our best manager ever.

When I was assistant to Allner at Kidderminster Harriers he passed a lot of that knowledge on to me.

That is how football should work in the building of knowledge of the game.

I am also pleased that the story has been told by veteran journalist Chris Bishop, who is Worcestershire born-and-bred, a man I have known for more than a decade. He grew up on non-League football in Worcestershire and his love for the game is akin to mine.

Let us look forward to a brighter future for Worcester City as the club climbs back to where it should be: a place among the top League sides in the country.

John Barton, Worcester City, Stourbridge, Kidderminster Harriers, Everton and Derby County.

Prologue

NON-LEAGUE FOOTBALL is a cruel game when you have no money. It is crueller when you have no ground. It is at its cruellest when you have neither.

This was the backdrop to a bleak close season for Worcester City in 2023 when the club simply didn't have two pennies to rub together.

For years, people in the pubs of Worcester had stood by and watched the club flounder in freefall. The so-called Faithful City looked on as fickle football destroyed what was once the most feared non-League club in the land. A club which once downed the mighty Liverpool before 15,000 people.

'Shame, it is sad to see,' they'd say over a pint.

'I remember there was 4,000 of us down there, on a Monday night, against Lockheed Leamington,' the older ones would say.

I used to feel sad every time I saw the photograph in the back bar of the Pheasant in New Street, Worcester, of Paul Moss taking a shot in the FA Cup first round replay at St George's Lane in 1983 before more than 5,000 fans. I was there that night and Moss, the flying accountant, ran all over Aldershot. It all seemed so distant and sad.

I knew the writing was on the wall back in March 2022, when I took my dad to see Worcester City play Bewdley Town at Ribbesford Meadows – basically a tiny football club on the fringes of a forest. I had just returned to Worcestershire after 27 years working away as a journalist in Africa and I wanted to get back into the non-League game, which was a big part of my roots.

I saw one of my mates from the old days.

'We are a fan-owned club,' he said sadly, 'but we have got no money and no ground, and we are going nowhere.'

Something had to happen.

So, when I covered a story, in the summer of 2023, about Worcester City's new owner Simon Lancaster, I was taken with the story. Here was a plain-speaking, modest man of Worcester who was prepared to put his money where his mouth was. At long last someone stood up to be counted. This was no fly-by-night asset-stripper; this was a man who had grown up with the club and watched it with his grandfather; as I had done.

I wanted to follow the story and the club across Worcestershire and the West Country to see this historic season of rebuilding play out.

I did this as a paying customer, with all the distance and impartiality that brings. I also wanted to contribute my money to the game I love. When I was growing up the skills, technique and courage I learned as a player came from simply watching non-League players close up.

It is a fascinating time to take the temperature of non-League football in this crazy world we live in – a chance to assess its place in our society and folk history at a time when the nation appears to be struggling with its identity.

Then again, I thought, this is a bigger story of three clubs who have been playing each other for more than 120 years: Worcester City; Stourbridge (the club which spawned Jude Bellingham); and Kidderminster Harriers.

Don't forget, it was artisans from the industrial Black Country, just north of Stourbridge, who brought the game with them to Worcestershire when they trekked south in search of work during the economic depressions of the late 19th century.

Three proud clubs battling the strange economic conditions of a tough world and struggling to stay alive, progress and stay relevant. It is an increasingly complicated and expensive world full of regulations and egos; where clubs are in a constant battle to find grounds, build grounds, or merely stop people from bulldozing them to make way for houses.

Three clubs who also share generations of players and managers. I also wanted to bring out the history and context of these clubs.

Non-League football has played a big part in my life since I saw my first game, with my father and grandfather, at the age of seven. With the wonders of the internet, it helped keep me in touch with my family and roots in nearly 30 years of working overseas.

This was a book I was born to write, but it so nearly didn't happen.

In February, I was despatched to do a few weeks of war reporting in Ukraine. It was a hard, uncomfortable slog chronicling the suffering of a nation at war. As far as I am aware I am one of the few people from Worcester to have spent his birthday in an air raid shelter in Odesa as Russian drones rained down on the city.

On the way through Heathrow, I mislaid my laptop with all my interviews and research on Worcester City. Thank heavens for Heathrow lost property. Right now, I am typing on that elusive laptop.

I am also thanking my lucky stars. It was a privilege to speak to so many passionate people in non-League football and I hope I have done them justice.

Clearly, this book was meant to be.

Chapter 1

Faithful City – seriously?

WORCESTER IS a blessed city which could have been built for a postcard. The tower of its mighty cathedral dominates the many church spires over the elegant palisades of the Georgian bridge over the River Severn.

The bridge itself looks more Paris than provincial England, and glows with lamplight at night which shimmers on the dark ripples of the river.

For centuries, many have called Worcester the Faithful City because of its spurious reputation as a city with Royalist sympathies.

To this day, the footballers of Worcester City wear the word Faithful on their shirts.

Yet faith has been in short supply at the once mighty club, in its dramatic fall from grace.

In the successful 1970s, many around the country asked why a city of Worcester's size – more than 100,000 inhabitants – didn't have a Football League club. Burnley has fewer people yet managed to sustain a Premier League side.

It is not as if the club had not earned their stripes. Just over a decade ago, Worcester City dumped Coventry City out of the FA Cup.

In 1959, the blue-and-white-striped footballers of the Faithful City humbled the reds of Liverpool, in the same competition, on their way to becoming one of the most feared non-League sides in the land.

So why faithful? The history books tell us this jewel set in the green Worcestershire countryside has proved a magnet for the royals for nearly a thousand years.

When wicked King John, of Robin Hood and Magna Carta fame, was on his death bed in Newark Castle, Nottingham, one of his last thoughts was about Worcester.

The dying king, in the throes of dysentery, ordered his courtiers to haul his corpse south and bury it in the nave of Worcester Cathedral, where he lies to this day. He had spent a few merry Christmases in Worcester and days of happy hunting in the thick forest that once hemmed in the walled city.

The city draws tourists and royals alike. You can't go to Worcester without marvelling at the winding sweep of the River Severn, with its brilliant white bevy of swans gliding the green waters.

For the people of Worcester, for centuries, the river was life. A source of food, water, trade and transport.

From chugging barges carrying chocolate crumb to Cadbury in Bournville, Birmingham, to silk and spices shipped in from distant shores and hauled up the river by Severn trows.

These small, sailed, cargo boats traded with ocean-going ships calling at the port of Bristol at the mouth of the Severn.

The graceful gliding swans' idyll may draw the tourists, but they belie the deadly undercurrents of the Severn which have snuffed out many a life.

Maybe, a dark metaphor for the precarious condition of senior football in the city.

Also, in recent years, Severn Trent Water Authority has been under fire for the amount of sewage lurking beneath the swans – there, maybe, another metaphor.

The city skyline is ever dominated by Worcester Cathedral. It sits on a shelf above Britain's longest river.

The cathedral is a monument to faith and hard work. It took generations of Worcester craftsmen hundreds of years to smooth and sculpt the massive stone blocks hauled with muscle and rope from quarries miles away and floated down the river. Fathers passed the skills down to their sons in backyard workshops scattered across the city. The fruit of this labour survived wars, plagues and the Reformation.

Wherever you go in Worcester, the imposing Gothic tower peeps over the rooftops, trees and black-and-white buildings of the ancient city. It is the abiding symbol of the administrative capital of Worcestershire – home to more than 600,000 people in this sleepy green corner of the industrial Midlands.

Every Monday night, like clockwork, the mighty bells of the cathedral ring out over the lush green of Chapter Meadows, where cattle graze on the opposite bank of the River Severn.

On summer nights, it is a sound and sight to behold as the bells peal over meadows stretching towards the hump-backed Malvern Hills on the horizon. A gorgeous view little changed for more than a thousand years.

The sound of the bells blended with the thumping flurry of wings as swans take flight on a clear summer's night is almost heavenly.

Wherever my dangerous assignments in journalism took me in Africa – that was a scene which I could close my eyes and savour. It sustained me in the worst of times, in the filthiest of cells.

On a mission from God, Benedictine monks founded an order at the cathedral in the 10th century. They were called the black monks, because of their dark habits. In 1501, the monks brought a bit of light to Worcester in the shape of four prized cygnets bought for 13 shillings and four pence – many times the cost of a flock of sheep.

For years, the black monks kept the white swans as pets in a pool in the cathedral grounds.

Then came all the king's men, armed to the teeth.

The split from Rome meant a nationwide purge of Catholic buildings. The soldiers of Henry VIII destroyed the priory in Worcester, in 1540, as part of the dissolution of the monasteries during the Reformation.

The fleeing monks turned the swans free into the nearby River Severn where they've survived, just, for more than 400 years.

Careless fishermen almost wiped them out in the 1970s. They tossed lead weights and nylon fishing wire into the waters that almost strangled and choked the swans into extinction.

A ban on discarding fishing gear into the river saw the swans recover, from a handful, into a bevy big enough to block the river with a fleet of white feathers.

Henry VIII's daughter, Elizabeth I, made a much more graceful and peaceful entry on horseback into Worcester on 16 August 1575, a warm and rainy summer's night, according to contemporary accounts.

It was part of her frequent and popular royal progress around the country on horseback. In modern parlance you could call it a PR tour.

By royal decree, the citizens of Worcester painted their houses with white-lime and lit torches, lanterns and candles in the fading light.

Thousands cheered as Queen Bess emerged, riding side saddle as ever, from under the turreted Foregate that stood guarding the road through the forest to the north of the city. She had spent the previous night in the village of Hartlebury, ten miles north, as a guest of the Bishop of Worcester.

Legend has it that her entourage stopped at the Rose and Crown in Hartlebury – now a home – in what is still called Inn Lane to raise a pint with astonished villagers on a hot August afternoon. She very likely did – there were very few places that she could have gone to on her way to a night at Hartlebury Castle.

The next day, in Worcester, torch bearers flanked her as she trotted slowly into the city. At the Cross, in the heart of the city, she stopped and turned her horse deftly 360 degrees – like a modern-day dressage rider – so all could see her.

Eyewitness accounts say she spoke from the saddle to plough boys and patricians alike.

On her way into the Faithful City, Queen Bess saw a couple of black pear trees that historians think, maybe, were planted hastily for the occasion. She decreed that three black pears should be incorporated into the crest of the city.

Nearly 450 years later the black pears remain on the city coat of arms and the badges of the footballers of Worcester City.

Aside from pears, war has been as much a part of the history of the city as royalty. The two often arrived in Worcester hand-in-hand; the people who ran the country fortified Worcester as far back as the Romans.

In the dark days of 1940, the British government saw Worcester as its Alamo if the Germans invaded.

The king was expected to move to Worcestershire, with his ministers setting up government in Worcester, as the city braced for a bloody last stand against the Nazis.

The army readied heavy guns on the roofs of buildings overlooking the Severn. Anti-tank guns were even in the back garden of the Bishop's Palace, the residence of the Bishop of Worcester.

The River Severn was seen as the last line of defence against the German panzers in a plan that could have been hatched by Captain Mainwaring of *Dad's Army*.

The British army figured that Hitler's tanks couldn't cross the river. They thought they were likely to try to force their way into the city down New Road, past the cricket ground, and across the 18th-century stone bridge over the Severn.

So, soldiers set explosive charges in the trees lining New Road. They set the charges in such a way that the trees would fall into the road and block the path of the panzers. Then more charges would blow the palisades off the sides of the bridge so the guns could have a clear field of fire against any troops, or tanks, who had the audacity to try to cross.

Thankfully, the panzers never turned up to test the theory. You can't help thinking the Wehrmacht would have found a way around this defence.

Fire, fury and fortifications were at the heart of Worcester's strongest link to Royalist sympathies in a war that many say gave rise to the Faithful City tag.

Worcester saw the first and last shots of the English Civil War in the 17th century. A bitter conflict that divided families and killed around 200,000 soldiers and civilians, a loss to the population proportionate to that of World War One.

The first shots came in a skirmish between dashing cavalier commander Prince Rupert of the Rhine and a 1,000-horse against around 1,000 Parliamentary dragoons. It happened at Powick Bridge just south of the city on 23 September 1642; it lasted 15 minutes, cost around 30 lives, and went down in history.

You could argue Worcester was among the first to declare for the Royalist cause and the last to surrender the fight for the crown at the Battle of Worcester in 1651.

The city also held out for the king under two months of siege in 1646 where the Faithful City name took root.

For months 5,000 Parliamentarian besiegers fired shots into the city held by Governor Colonel Henry Washington, a relative of the first US President George Washington. His 1,500-strong garrison gave a good account of themselves sallying beyond the city walls for skirmishes. In one short, sharp clash, in what is now Cripplegate Park on the banks of the Severn, they captured a couple of Parliamentarian battle flags.

The next morning, the Royalist defenders hung the flags from the Cathedral tower to taunt the besiegers about this defeat. Football-style mind games, 17th-century style.

The Parliamentarians fought back with bullets and their own brand of mind games, shouting: 'Washington's bastards!' and 'Papist pigs!' across the river.

In these hungry and desperate days, legend has it that the defenders painted, in Latin, on the drawbridge of the bridge over the river: *'City Fidelis Deo et Rege'* (City faithful to God and King).

Words that also found their way on to the city's coat of arms, and the badge of the football club, which carries the legend: *'Civitas in bello et pace fidelis'*. A city faithful in peace and war.

Eventually, the Parliamentary forces bombarded and starved out the defenders and the poor city folk who suffered with them. You can be sure faith and love for the royals were wearing a bit thin by the end of the siege.

Tempestuous times tested the faith of the people of Worcester, even more, in the final battle of the English Civil War. A story I learned at my mother's knee.

On a glorious August morning in 1651, a slender 21-year-old with long black curly hair rode into the city knowing it was crown or coffin for him.

The man, who was to become Charles II, had marched from Scotland at the head of around 16,000 Scottish soldiers determined to reclaim the throne.

Historians believe Oliver Cromwell and his Parliamentarian army merely shadowed the invading Royalist army; allowing troops to advance deeply into England, closing off escape and supply routes, so he could surround them and wipe them out.

The young claimant to the throne arrived in Worcester the day after his troops. Royals always knew how to make an entrance into Worcester; the crowds feted Charles, and the mayor held the civic sword high above his head as he led the future monarch to the Cross in the heart of the city. Here Charles was proclaimed as the King of England, Scotland and Wales.

Charles hoped a solid victory at Worcester would spark a Royalist uprising and bring people to his colours to unseat Cromwell and his po-faced puritan Republican regime.

Think again. If anything people ran from the royal colours; there was an embarrassing call for recruits on Pitchcroft, just outside the city, which drew a mere handful.

This is where the Faithful City narrative starts to look a bit queasy. People in Worcestershire were tried of looting, raping armies marching through their land; they wanted peace – no matter who was winning – and didn't want to have the expense and pain of garrisoning hungry, thirsty, troublesome soldiers.

In short, Cromwell took Worcester in a ruthless pincer movement. As his forces swept through Sidbury gate, from the south of the walled city, many of the Scottish defenders threw down their weapons. The sweating and bloody Charles II made an impassioned plea to his beaten troops.

'I would sooner you kill me now, than allow me to see the consequences of this day.'

You can imagine, in the confusion, some of his soldiers may have considered it. Charles fled the city out of the back door of his digs in New Street as the London dragoons kicked down the front door; his soldiers died in their hundreds so the narrow streets of Worcester were blocked by the bodies of men and horses.

So faithful?

Adrian Gregson, former Mayor of Worcester, once told the Battle of Worcester Society: 'I think the people of Worcester were faithful, but only to whoever was in charge!'

I rest my case.

Chapter 2

New Season, Fresh Start

'SEE THAT?' said one of the stewards, in his high visibility jacket, leaning forward and pointing as I walked through the gate at Claines Lane for the first game of the season.

I saw the team in their new training kit warming up with a dozen pristine footballs in front of the nets.

'That is the club's entire assets in one picture!'

We both laughed. We non-League fans share this gallows humour. You don't have to have it, but it helps.

For this was the season that almost wasn't for a club so famous people had heard of it up and down the land, yet, so broke that it almost packed up altogether after 121 years of proud history.

1 August 2023, backed by a new owner, was as much a relief as it was full of the promise of optimism for a new season.

Undoubtedly, this season was going to be a landmark one that could bode well, or ill, for the survival of Worcester City.

The weather wasn't much help. We were still in the depths of summer, yet overhead there were dark, threatening skies. It had been one of the wettest Julys on record.

On the way to one of the pre-seasons friendlies, a few weeks earlier, I nearly drowned in torrential rain and ended up taking refuge in the New Inn, in Claines, to dry out before taking a taxi home. Unreal. This was the first game of the season and the dark clouds sat, like a bruise, on the beautiful view from the commanding heights of Claines Lane, Worcester City's temporary home which the club rents from the Worcestershire Football Association.

From a vantage point behind the goal, you can look over the trees to the beautiful Malvern Hills curled up on the horizon like a giant hump-backed creature.

It was more than half an hour before the season kicked off and small groups of elderly, balding men were gathering and chatting by the fence around the pitch.

Next to me stood another of the volunteer stewards who keep clubs like Worcester City running, in shorts under his high-visibility jacket. With his arms behind his back, he rocked from side to side, and I felt he wanted to say something to me.

'You know what,' he said.

'I chose to retire in July so I could enjoy the best of the weather.'

He paused for effect.

'I don't know why I bothered!'

We both smiled. It was the kind of deadpan Worcestershire humour I missed in the 30 years I was travelling the world as a journalist. As I said, this kind of humour helps when you support a non-League club. I asked the steward who we were playing in first game. Honestly, I had no clue, and neither did he.

'Hold on a minute.'

He walked away for a brief conversation with a nearby group of elderly men and came back within minutes.

'Apparently its Tuffley Rovers,' said the steward checking my blank expression in return.

'That is how far we have fallen,' said the steward, with another expression somewhere between irritation and resignation.

Tuffley Rovers, from Gloucester, was founded by a boot and shoe repairer in 1929. Its first headquarters was in an old railway carriage parked in Stroud Road, Tuffley, where you could buy a season ticket and get your shoes mended at the same time.

Most of the life of Tuffley Rovers was spent in the Gloucester County leagues. For the club, believe it or not, the lowly Hellenic League is the giddy heights.

The most famous part of Tuffley Rovers is its manager. Neil Mustoe has been at the helm since 2021. He was at Manchester United, along with Phil Neville, Robbie Savage and Brian McClair, before moving to Wigan Athletic and Cambridge United. He returned to the city of his birth to make nearly 400 appearances for Gloucester City in its rise from the Southern League to the National League.

Twenty minutes later the teams emerged for the first game of the season in the Hellenic League. Arguably, the lowest level a Worcester City team had ever played in.

Tuffley Rovers, in their maroon kit, ran out looking a bit like a good Sunday morning team. One or two looked a bit portly, nearly all looked heavy on their feet.

Tuffley Rovers had clearly read the reports about the rejuvenated Worcester City. One or two of the players looked apprehensive and from the first kick of the game the visitors appeared determined to hold out for a draw.

Worcester City pressed early in the game. A cross from the right was headed just wide by centre-forward Kyle Belmonte to a smattering of applause a bit like a Sunday afternoon cricket match. The first gate of the season was to be a modest 487 and sounded a little subdued.

Minutes later City were heading a Tuffley Rovers attempt off their line.

Under the orange sunset Worcester City pressed and pressed for a breakthrough, missing a couple of sitters along the way. The Tuffley keeper made a couple of blinding saves to keep the scores level.

Then came the chicanery which turns me savage. As a paying customer of non-League football all I ask for is honest effort, no cheating and no pathetic time-wasting by the goalkeeper.

The season before, I had watched a young, promising goalkeeper for Bedford Town mess up his side's survival chances with time-wasting tactics. Bedford, struggling against relegation, went 1-0 up away from home.

The young keeper proceeded to waste time with almost comic earnestness. Slowly, slowly jogging around the back of the goal to take goal kicks from the opposite side. Spending two minutes digging a little mound from which to take that goal kick. Yawn. Standing like a statue over the kick for another minute. Rolling around on the floor feigning injury. Rolling the ball from one side of the area to the other. Angry yawn. I yearn for the day when referees get tough and stamp out this kind of gamesmanship once and for all.

To cut a long boring story short. The Bedford Town goalkeeper succeeded in slowing down the game, instead of keeping the supply of balls to his forwards, giving them a chance to score a second and secure three badly needed points.

The opposition took advantage of the slowdown in play, scored two goals and won the game 2-1.

That is why the Tuffley Rovers keeper Luke Merchant drew jeers from the sidelines when he blatantly tried to slow down the game and waste time. It seemed Tuffley Rovers had decided from the kick-off they were going home with one point by running down the clock.

It was a shame to see Merchant, a man mountain of a goalkeeper who had made sterling saves during the game, messing about. A good keeper who not only commands his penalty area, but also looks like he could command a spot on *Love Island*.

The biggest cheer of the night came when the referee booked Merchant for time-wasting.

It kind of summed up the goalless night, but the booking was far too late to influence the game; a common mistake referees make.

Clearly it was going to be a struggle in this season of reconstruction and salvation.

It was going to be a stern test for Worcester City and their loyal, long-suffering, supporters.

As the ball bobbled around the Tuffley Rovers penalty area I said: 'Where's Paul Moss when you need him?'

One or two of the older supporters smiled knowingly at the memory of Moss, the flying accountant, who scored for fun in the early 1980s at St George's Lane.

On the way out of the ground, I was thinking of my walk through the city to Claines Lane earlier in the day.

The mid-summer air over the River Severn was low and sweet.

Black clouds threatened overhead, but Britain's longest river was welcoming, warm and tranquil. As I walked along the bank on the way to the first Worcester City game of the season I was looking for a metaphor from a river both beautiful and treacherous.

I leaned against the railing on the city side of the river. When I was a child, the elders used to warn us not to swim in the River Severn with its whirlpools and vicious undercurrents that can suck you under in a second.

'If you go in there, you don't come out!' they used to say. I have always held affection and respect for the beauty and power of the swift Severn.

My father and more than ten generations before him, for at least 500 years, were born in the Worcestershire town of Bewdley on the banks of the Severn. I was born in Stourport-on-Severn three miles away and a hop, skip and a jump from the river.

When my daughter was born in Africa, a world away from Worcestershire, in the heat of an African summer's night I named her Saberne – one of the ancient names for the river – in honour of the waterway that fed and watered our family for centuries.

When she grew up I told her stories of the river Goddess Sabrina, one of the modern versions of the name, who was thrown into the waters to end a civil war. The elders used to tell us, when we were kids, that you could see her spirit on the river on misty mornings, even though in truth, I never saw anything.

I figured my daughter may have been born in Brixton, in Johannesburg the City of Gold, South Africa, far from home and was likely to travel the world, which she did. I wanted her name to remind her of her ancestors and where they were from.

As I smiled at the memory, a bird swooped down and plucked a fish from the river. It dropped the fish as soon as it fluttered clear of the brown waters of the Severn.

The determined bird hovered over the grey-brown water; it dived and nipped the fish with its beak. Again, it dropped and hovered back. Again, and again.

The bird must have dropped the fish and swooped down to pick it up eight or nine times before flying off low across the river with its morsel. If at first, you don't succeed.

It never fails. When a writer looks for a clear-cut and apt metaphor, mother nature can deliver one, as sure as a sunrise, to remember for the rest of your days.

The bird was Worcester City and football was the fish. It mirrored the struggle of the city to cling on to the remains of its football pride against bankruptcy and apathy.

Worcester must be one of the most pleasant walks to a football ground in English football. Aside from the splendour of the river and cathedral, nature is never far away. A 30-minute walk, either way, from the heart of the city, home to more than 100,000 people, and you are back in forests and open fields.

The loud dawn chorus is never drowned out by traffic and every now and again you can catch a glimpse of foxes and squirrels darting through the streets.

One night, my daughter and I saw a young wild deer; it could have been from nearby Perry Wood overlooking the city, running through the streets trying to find its way home. You could tell it was feral as it mistook the shop windows for escape routes and kept running into them. It was a sad sight; each window promising freedom and then delivering a bump to the head.

Another metaphor from nature, as Worcester City embarked on a great escape from the winding streets of football obscurity.

Chapter 3

Non-League and Me

A LOT of people who claim to support big, powerful clubs by merely watching them on television laugh at non-League supporters who take a close, lifelong, interest in the game. Never going to win anything, they say, never going to qualify for Europe, never going to pay £100m for a footballer etc. Yawn.

I laugh back safe in the knowledge that the non-League game, if you put the time and effort into experiencing it, is a rich slice of English life.

A Saturday afternoon theatre of raw emotion. Take the third round of the FA Trophy. Stourbridge – my first love – against AFC Telford.

We old hands thought all was lost; 2-1 down and time up.

Then, a rapid break down the left wing; I thought the winger's legs were going to fly off. He crossed the ball to Montel Gibson, who drilled it into the bottom left-hand corner; within seconds another break down the left and a lancing pass to Gibson, who smashed it at the keeper. The ball spilled from the goalie's grasp to the feet of Stourbridge striker Reece Styche. It seemed like the world stood still as he clipped it into the top corner. Cue several hundred grown men leaping around like teenagers.

At the final whistle, we sauntered back around the cinder bank. Everyone was happy, turning to each other, smiling, laughing; reliving the moment; saying it was a million to one chance that the keeper spilled the ball on to the exact divot to set it up for Styche. How it would never happen again in a million years.

We were, as a great football writer once put it, on holiday from life. Sweet.

The best bit was, there was no commentator shouting in our ears, telling us what we should think. No one was worried about statistics, nor a VAR check, nor passing rates, nor transfer targets; no one was tweeting idiotic abuse. No one was treating the game like it was an A Level subject.

All we could see was the game we'd all played and loved and nothing else, plain and simple honest-to-God grassroots football.

All thanks to a non-League team who played brave, passing football, for tuppence halfpenny, in the terms of the modern game; playing as if their lives depended upon it. What you get in return for a tenner in most non-League grounds.

Players who work during the week like the rest of us, drink in the same pubs and who live not in a mansion, but in a modest house not too far away.

Players who get home at 3am from an away game and get up for work the next morning – like the rest of us.

This was the non-League world I was born into.

I saw my first game at my grandfather's knee, a few yards from the spot where Styche knocked in the winner.

That first game was on August Bank Holiday Monday 1970 and Kidderminster Harriers played away at Stourbridge.

My grandfather Eric Hunt Bishop, a big, strong-handed carpenter, had been watching Kidderminster Harriers since the 1930s. He took my father Tony Bishop, in 1946, when football restarted after the war, with thousands flocking back to the grounds desperate to feel normal again.

Also, at that August Bank Holiday game, was my father Tony reporting on it as part of his new job on the *Wolverhampton Express and Star*.

Stourbridge is on the fringes of the so-called Black Country, the crucible of the Industrial Revolution that created wealth and left the buildings black with smoke. On that night my grandfather told me of my Black Country roots; how my great-grandfather, William Grainger, had been a blacksmith's striker just down the road in Netherton, and had chucked in this industrial life to buy a farm near Bewdley, in Worcestershire, even though he didn't know one end of a cow from the other. The family farms there to this day.

This was August 1970, a summer for reflection on lost glories. A couple of months before England exited the World Cup, by losing 3-2 to West Germany in the quarter-final after being 2-0 up. In our tiny corner of Worcestershire, it felt like a bereavement.

This golden evening, with a strawberry sunset, felt like a new beginning.

Youthful John Chester – with a beard and moves to match – stood out like a Worcestershire George Best, as be glided through Stourbridge's leaden-footed defence.

It ended 2-1 to the Harriers. Peter Wassall scored the winner, one of the staggering 395 goals he scored in 541 games for Kidderminster Harriers. Meanwhile his brother Brendon, a classy midfielder who should have played at a much higher level, carpeted out some of the most sumptuous passes non-League football had ever seen.

The Wassall brothers scored 663 goals in 1,227 appearances for Kidderminster Harriers in ten years of loyalty and application. How any non-League club, worth its salt, would kill for that kind of service and results in this fickle day and age.

At the end of the game the three generations of my family met up near the players' entrance.

'I think they needed one more goal ... to be sure,' said my grandfather. Thank heaven, no talk then of high press, or low block, or false nine. Thank heaven.

Three weeks later, I saw Worcester City for the first time in an FA Cup game at Kidderminster Harriers. There were 3,391 people there and the noise was deafening. I had grown up in a small Worcestershire village of a few hundred and had never seen that many people. Worcester City lost 1-0.

My grandfather, with a gentle voice as deep as the ocean, always used to romanticise about the FA Cup; calling it the 'English Cup' and invoking the Victorian founders of Association Football. He told me if Kidderminster Harriers won another ten games the club would get to Wembley. I was seven; it didn't sound difficult, I believed.

When Kidderminster Harriers got through to the fourth qualifying round away at Hereford United, I remember taking the car journey with my father and grandfather; it was like going to the other side of the world. At the end of it was another huge, intimidating crowd of nearly 7,000 – more people than I had seen in my entire life! It was a 5-0 thrashing at the hands of Hereford; it could have been 10. Rarely have I seen 11 men so vulnerable and shell-shocked. The brutal shattering of the English Cup dream was a very early lesson in life for a seven-year-old.

As we left, early, we could hear the crowd roaring: 'We want six!'

I looked up to my grandfather's face under his trilby with a feather in the band. He laughed, shook his head and looked down at me with a smile: 'Only a game.'

That was my baptism; it was almost too much too soon. I drifted away from the game for a few years. When I came back to non-League football it was with a vengeance watching every game I could at Worcester City, Stourbridge and Kidderminster Harriers.

In August, in my teenage years, as the nights drew in with a nip, I used to emerge from my parents' house in Hartlebury, look at the floodlights of Kidderminster Harriers on the horizon and head for the next bus into town.

On the way through the garden, I would pluck a ripe James Greaves apple from the tree and put it into my pocket along with 20 pence for the bus and 20 pence to get into the ground.

The bus would stop at Hoobrook and I would run up the hill to dash through the turnstiles as the whistle blew. I would sit on the concrete wall around the ground and eat my apple while listening to the music of players calling, exhorting and chastising each other. I was the happiest teenager on the planet. In these stressing, depressing, times, it is a comfort to hold such sweet and simple memories.

Sadly, my paternal grandfather died in 1972. Thankfully my maternal grandfather took an interest in non-League football in his retirement. This kept up the three-generation trips on Saturday afternoons and Tuesday nights; looking back, I never knew how lucky I was.

My maternal grandfather, Ernest Nash, was a man of Kent and as hard as nails. He was an ex-serviceman and civil servant who had been evacuated to Worcestershire with my grandmother and mother during the war.

'He got it!' he used to say with a face which took decades off him, after one of our star strikers had run through and scored.

Of poorer players, grandpa would grimace, shake his head and say: 'Wouldn't pay him in washers!'

Together we journeyed to Worcester City, Kidderminster Harriers and Stourbridge.

In the week, we talked injuries and who we felt should be in the team. Dad would come home with animated stories about the latest signings and club news.

On Saturdays, the three of us would travel to Worksop, Taunton Town, Forest Green, Tamworth, Merthyr Tydfil and Enfield. In these times, we would have called it bonding; back then it was just fun family outings full of chat, fish, chips and laughter.

When I grew up to become a journalist, I covered non-League games for the newspapers where I cut my teeth, including the *Kidderminster Shuttle* and the *County Express*. It taught me a lot about life and politics.

If the team won handsomely supporters would say: 'Great report, young man!'

If they didn't and you wrote a critical piece you would hear: 'You watched a bloody different game from me last week. It was Nicholls who flicked it on for the first goal, I was five yards from it, and you never mentioned it? What kind of a journalist are you?'

When I left Worcestershire on my way up in journalism, my father used to ring me after games to let me know the scores and posted me newspaper cuttings. Wherever I was, in Darlington or Cote d'Ivoire, it was comforting and made me feel closer to my family and home.

I spent more than 30 years travelling the world as a journalist. Along the way I was lucky enough to watch top-flight football in a dozen countries. I saw a Brazilian score for Al-Hilal in Khartoum, watched Kaizer Chiefs in Johannesburg, Miramar in New Zealand, Dynamos in Zimbabwe and Desportivo de Maputo in Mozambique.

Yet, I have more laughs, happier times and more fun and banter on English non-League grounds than I have had at all of the big grounds combined.

Non-League football has influenced my life for the better and is bound up with my humanity and roots. I am glad it was a part of my life and countless millions of others in the land of my birth. Long may it live and prosper.

Chapter 4

City Slickers

WORCESTER CITY supporters. You couldn't ignore them when I was growing up.

In the grey world of non-League football in the 1970s and 1980s, Worcester City fans stood out from the rest.

They seemed to have that confidence and swagger that was in short supply in those dowdy days. They were loud, vocal and didn't care what people thought of them.

The first time I ran into them was at Villa Park in the final of the Birmingham Senior Cup in the spring of 1976.

I was impressed by how they seemed to fill the vast empty stadium with fewer than 1,000 people in it. How they sang and backed Worcester City to a hard-fought 1-0 win over a tough Stourbridge side. Record goalscorer John Inglis got the winner at the Holte End.

The majority of supporters were those too old, too young, or too infirm to follow the crowd to the Wolves or Albion, just down the road.

In those days, it may have been only 25 pence to watch a Southern League game, but you could still see top-flight football for under a quid. The majority of supporters were stoic old men dressed in thick, long, wool coats which appeared bullet-proof, evoking the lean post-war years. They greeted goals with a terse 'yes' and a brief clap.

Many of the grey elders grumbled about how it was a better game in the old days when you could buy humbugs for a halfpenny on the terraces, while watching the centre-forward get his dislocated shoulder shoved back into place and sent back into the fray. No substitutes then.

'Didn't we get some gates, eh?' someone would say of the old days.

'We did, Stanley; and the players those days weren't afraid of messing up their hair!'

Cue laughter and more talk about the paucity of skill on the pitch. Especially when another corner went to waste.

'Johnny Hancocks used to score from the corner flag!'

Nobody could dispute that, but then again Hancocks was a professional footballer who trained all week and played for Wolverhampton Wanderers. Whereas the bloke who just took the corner had emptied the bins for the council the day before.

This was how the non-League game struggled to garner attention in the 1970s and 1980s.

Free-to-air football on colour television and cheaper tickets for top-flight games meant that glamour was within easy reach of the working man.

You have to remember this was the era when football was not as fashionable as it is now; where people who don't know Bobby Moore from Patrick Moore claim 'lifelong' fandom.

Back in the day, when I was a young journalist, I went to a party on Saturday night where a young woman asked me what I had done in the day. I replied I had been to the football.

'Ugh, how anti-social,' she said turning up her nose.

If that conversation had happened this year, the same person would have told me how they had supported Manchester City since before they were born and had admiration for the team's high press and ability to track back in defence.

Worcester City supporters were the antidote to all that. They knew and loved the game and moved in big groups, in the successful late 1970s, they had that bluster about them.

I remember vividly the first time I watched a game among them at Aggborough, the home of Kidderminster Harriers in the Southern League Cup, in the autumn of 1977.

I was 14 and hungry for football. I badgered my father, late in the day, to take me to the game so we were late for the kick-off.

As we hurried across the car park, past the parked coaches from Worcester, I heard Harriers fans singing: 'Easy! Easy! Easy!'

Harriers had scored in the first minute against the visitors from Worcester and a higher division. As we walked into the ground Mush Davies made it 2-0 with a low shot past the right hand of the Worcester City keeper under the dim floodlights, which weren't great. They had illuminated the first ever floodlit FA Cup match in history in September 1955 when Kidderminster Harriers beat Brierley Hill Alliance 4-2 in a replay. Legend has it that the Harriers directors had to climb the pylons to diffuse the lights with a bucket of whitewash.

Under the lights you could just about see only the wings were green. In those days, the centre of the pitch and goalmouths were churned-up mud from the first few weeks of the season. Few clubs devoted much time to maintaining their pitches.

'You see, Kiddy, they'm, getting these!' said one of the disgruntled Worcester supporters in front of me in front of the tea hut, at the side of the pitch, as Worcester almost went 3-0 down. He seemed to think his team weren't getting enough of the ball to Dave Roberts on the wing.

Every time Roberts made a dashing run, it seemed the other players ignored him and switched the ball to the opposite flank. Roberts would hold out his hands in complaint.

'Davy Roberts, Davy Roberts!' said the bearded elder pointing, turning to his mates and jumping up and down to make his point.

'Come on Lionel!' said a grey old man, who must have been in his 70s, every 30 seconds just behind me; in between puffs on his cigarette.

Lionel Martin was a rock, as usual, in the thick of midfield. People used to say he sometimes hung on to the ball for too long. This was largely because most opponents were too scared to take it off him. I was impressed by how Worcester City fans roared their team on even though they were two down.

In the days when I reported on non-League for the weekly newspapers, away supporters could have fitted into one large car, especially if it was far and the weather was cold. Sometimes, when I was filing my stories, I would almost miss goals by the away team because there was virtually no noise, a quick handshake and a swift kick-off.

Worcester City, by contrast, always seemed to pull the crowds away with them, especially when they were winning.

OK, I was very impressionable in my teenage days, but it also seemed the City supporters were a lot more fashionably dressed than most inhabitants of non-League grounds in the Midlands.

From what I could overhear, most had either apprenticeships in the engineering firms, which employed thousands in Worcester in those days, or skilled jobs paying more than the average wage. They wore fashionable clothes I hadn't seen in the shops of Kidderminster.

They were also ready to put their money where their mouth was and often chipped in for new signings. Supporters raised £14,000 – a fortune back in 1963 – to build the impressive main stand at St George's Lane.

On this night, one or two supporters were arm-in-arm with young women. They looked adoringly at their men under the lights. In a break in play, there would be a passionate embrace.

Heck. This was romance that regulars at Kidderminster and Stourbridge saw little of.

The travelling fans seemed to get louder as the tide of the game turned. In the second half City pulled one back and then Dave Roberts erased his night of frustration on the wing by smashing home a penalty with ease. It was 2-2, all square and Kidderminster Harriers looked like a boxer out on his feet.

The only person standing in the way of a rampant Worcester City was the home goalkeeper Bryan Parry. He played for the Harriers for years and was probably one of the bravest and most agile keepers I ever saw.

On this night, he dived and parried and tipped against a flurry of shots from the rampant Worcester City forwards.

The moment that decided the game came as the referee checked his watch near the end.

There was a free kick just inside the Kidderminster half and Worcester City's Brian Kenning stood over it.

Kenning was a colossus of a player. He thundered across the park like a buffalo and possessed a cannonball of a shot.

As Kenning prepared for the kick, everyone was expecting it to be floated into the penalty area. Not a chance. With time running out Kenning took a short run-up and swung his mighty right leg through the ball. The crowd held its breath for a precious moment as the ball sailed through the air like a guided missile. Parry dived in vain, stretching and clawing, before crashing to the ground.

The ball rattled into the top left-hand corner and the away fans erupted. For the first time, I saw fans punching the air with clenched fists. Electricity on a damp Monday night in Worcestershire.

Two images summed up the last-gasp victory. Parry lay on the floor, like a bird with a broken wing, his bravery crushed. The game can be cruel.

I shall never forget Kenning running a huge circle of joy across the pitch with both hands making the V-for-victory sign. You could almost hear his heavy footsteps on the turf.

A year later, Kenning was gone, but that Worcester City passion – through relegation, ground sale and bankruptcy – lives on.

Chapter 5

Humble Beginnings

MORE THAN a century ago, Worcester City Football Club was born out of frustration, failure and penury in a smoke-filled pub backroom amid pint pots, big moustaches, cloth caps and bowler hats.

It was a humble beginning, before a sparse meeting, which the organisers said was a good sign of the lack of enthusiasm for senior football in the city. The birth took place in the Paul Pry, a small pub which stands to this day, in the Butts, just off Angel Place, a street through the busy heart of the city.

Worcester was a different city in 1902; trams swept through the city centre, steam trains blew their whistles a few times every hour and the outskirts of the city still rattled to the clip-clop of horse-drawn transport.

Many of the footballers in the city had returned that year from fighting the South African War. Worcestershire sent 2,000 soldiers to fight in South Africa, at the turn of the century – 222 never came back, according to regimental history. Those who did make it back were cheered home from the railway station by thousands. The city built a war memorial by Worcester Cathedral to commemorate those who didn't.

The Paul Pry was built on a street with both military and football connections. The Butts refers to archery butts that stood in a dry ditch just outside the city walls. They were put up in 1515. That was the year Henry VIII resurrected an ancient law enforcing archery practice on Sundays, under the eye of clergy, in preparation for war.

Like most young lads across the country the Worcester boys would have preferred to play a crude version of what we know today as football. On many Sundays they did so, on pain of death – that is how deeply football runs in our veins.

The Paul Pry was built, centuries later, to serve the nearby bustling cattle market. It was named after a fictitious character from a play described as a comical and meddlesome soul consumed by prying into people's lives.

The play enjoyed a popular run in 1826 at the Kings Head Theatre, the forerunner to the now demolished Theatre Royal in nearby Angel Street, a couple of hundred yards from the pub. It turned Paul Pry into a household name.

This success gave rise to names for at least one publication as well as a couple of Worcester pubs, in the hope of reflected glory.

In was in the autumn of 1902 that the Paul Pry staged its own drama that was to change the course of football in the city.

On 4 September, the pub hosted this small, yet crucial, gathering of football fans and portly pipe-smoking officials in bowler hats.

The chairman regretted the low turnout that didn't speak highly of the enthusiasm for senior football in the city, according to a report in the *Worcestershire Chronicle* of 6 September, entitled 'A Deadlock'.

The mood was one of defeat more than deadlock. On this night a failing football club would die and a new one rise from the ashes to write its name across English non-League football.

The club on life support was Berwick Rangers, founded more than a decade earlier in Worcester.

A bunch of Worcester lads, who likely would have dodged archery practice centuries before, are said to have founded the club following a chat under the streetlamps in the Bath Road in the 1880s.

The origin of the name is not clear; some say it was named after the Berwick Arms public house in Bath Road which is now a home; others that it was named after the Berwick Brook a free kick's distance away.

It was a time for action in the game. Football enthusiasts founded the Birmingham Football Association in 1875. Stourbridge Standard, one of the founders of the league, was formed a year later. Kidderminster Harriers joined in 1886 when it amalgamated with local rivals Kidderminster Olympic. Both started out as athletics clubs.

Unemployment in the industrial Black Country – always a hotbed of football – sent thousands of artisan ball players heading south into Worcestershire looking for work and taking the game with them.

Football clubs in the county, where the game was growing rapidly in popularity, were only too happy to find a job for these workers and offer them a few bob for playing on a Saturday.

The Football Association was only 12 years old at that time and it would be years before big names like Sheffield United, West Ham and Chelsea kicked a ball in anger.

Berwick Rangers joined the Birmingham League in 1893 and fought their way up from obscurity but didn't quite set the world on fire. *The Official History of Worcester City* has records going back only as far as the 1893/94 season. It shows modest progress rising to finishing fourth in 1897 in a nomadic existence, which saw the club play at: the Cinderella Ground in Northwick in the north of the city; Flagge Meadow, where Worcester Royal Grammar School now play; Worcestershire's cricket ground at New Road and Militia Meadow before settling on Severn Terrace next to the racecourse at Pitchcroft.

Severn Terrace is now the car park for the Swan Theatre, but in its footballing heyday it packed in thousands.

There were two teams in Worcester in the 1890s, even though there were questions over whether the city could support even one. Worcester Rovers were the bigger side and a clash for the pride of the city used to draw as many as 7,000 to see them play Berwick Rangers. People would travel from all over the county to pay a penny to cram into makeshift grounds.

Sadly, Rovers disbanded halfway through the 1899/1900 season following financial difficulties.

Berwick Rangers were in danger of following Rovers, which would have left the city bereft of senior football.

On this September evening in the Paul Pry, in 1902, Berwick Rangers were on borrowed time and borrowed money. If it had been a boxing ring, the club was bloodied and on the ropes.

The last few years of the 1890s had not been kind to Berwick Rangers. They had tumbled to the bottom of the Birmingham League and the money had run out. The directors – who claimed they had put £350 (nearly £50,000 in today's money) into the club – said they had done all they could and were ready to hand over.

The night before the Paul Pry meeting, supporters met at the Bell Hotel, a hundred yards away in Broad Street, to form a deficit committee to raise money.

Time was running out. Less than 48 hours later Berwick Rangers were to play their first game in the Birmingham League against Dudley at Severn Terrace. If the club failed to play, there would be a penalty of £10, money the club couldn't afford.

A stand-in secretary laid bare the parlous state of the finances of Berwick Rangers. He read out a letter of demands from the retreating directors to whomever had the bottle to take over the club: to pay £73, in cash within three months, for stands, fixtures and fittings, plus the players' kit; or the new club pay £30 rent to the trustees for the ground and also cover all rents and rates up to the end of the season in April; pay for the players' boots and shirts immediately to the tune of £7 10 shillings.

The deficit committee had spoken to the directors in the morning in search of better terms, but the idea had been 'pooh-poohed'.

The directors also said the boots and kit were worth more like £50.

'I shouldn't like to give £4 for them!' said a voice from the back to cries of 'Hear, hear'.

To laughter from the floor, one of the directors said he was very sorry for the players who were in the pawnshop.

Then came the act from the acting secretary that was to make history and create a name that was to be written across English non-League football.

The acting secretary was John William Green, aged 28. He was a young clerk for Midland Railways, living at 43 Ashcroft Road, in the Tything in St George's parish, with his wife and son George. I have checked the Census records and found only one JW Green in a city of 40,000 people. I am almost certain this was the man who took the sense of the meeting and proposed that the new club be called Worcester City Football Club. It was seconded by a C Hughes (I am afraid I couldn't find Mr Hughes in the Census) and went down in history.

Green, born in Blockhouse in St Paul's in Worcester, was standing in as secretary for Henry Lewis Rolfe, who couldn't take the chair because of 'certain complications' on the night, even though he attended the meeting. The *Worcestershire Chronicle* did not delve into the reason why.

The two young men worked together at Midland Railway headquarters, in Midland Road, near Worcester's Shrub Hill Station.

Rolfe, who was born in Swindon, had worked as a railway coach finisher, like his father before him. In the 1891 Census he was an apprentice coach finisher aged 15. By 1901, aged 25, Rolfe had transferred to Worcester. In 1900, he was married to Ellen Price, the daughter of a Worcester bootmaker, and had settled down in Rogers Hill in the north of the city.

I am convinced the two were friends. They were almost the same age; surely there must have been a good deal of trust between the two for Green to be allowed to stand in for such an important meeting.

Sadly, Green lived a very short life. In 1911, he died at the age of 39, leaving a wife and 14-year-old son.

Rolfe lived to a ripe old age, dying in 1952 at the age of 77. He was a stalwart of the administration of the club that was born on this night, spearheading its rebirth and the move to St George's Lane in 1905. He is in the early team photographs, an upstanding-looking man in bowler hat with a grand moustache.

Berwick Rangers played their penultimate game at Severn Terrace two days after the Paul Pry meeting, losing 2-0 to Dudley before a sparse crowd.

On 9 September, the following Tuesday, there was another crisis meeting, this time at the Duke of York Hotel, where directors elected to put the limited company into voluntary liquidation. On the same night, the club accepted the decision by the Birmingham League to allow the resignation of Berwick Rangers and enable a new club to take over the fixtures.

The final Berwick Rangers game in history came on Saturday, 13 September against title challengers Stourbridge at Amblecote. To the surprise of many, probably including themselves, Berwick Rangers signed off with a 3-1 victory bringing the curtain down on a decade of pioneering football in Worcester.

This game cleared the way for the first ever game for Worcester City Football Club. It kicked off at Severn Terrace before more than 1,000 fans on a fine autumn afternoon on Saturday, 20 September.

Worcester City took the lead early thanks to a long-range effort from inside-forward Len Ricketts, but Stafford soon equalised and scored the winner in a grim struggle in the second half.

A losing start that didn't get much better as the season wore on. City created some kind of record by losing four games in five days in April.

Worcester City won at home to Halesowen in the last game of the season near the end of April to avoid the ignominy of having to apply for re-election in the new club's first season in the Birmingham League. They finished 15th out of 18 clubs and didn't need to reapply.

Yet it was the dawn of a great club that would dominate the cream of English non-League football before thousands, for years, and would one day see off the mighty Liverpool.

Should there be a statue at the new ground to John William Green, the man who proposed the name that unleashed more than 122 glorious years of Worcester City? If Fulham could put up a statue to Michael Jackson, who had virtually nothing to do with the west London club, why not?

Chapter 6

Enter the Quiet White Knight

AS WHITE knights go, Simon Lancaster was as much home-grown as heaven-sent.

  He was born, as was his fortune, in Fernhill Heath, a small village just outside Worcester, on the road to Droitwich.

  It was on a depressing down day in his mother's back garden, that he turned an epiphany into a multi-million-pound business. A remarkable turnaround of fortune akin to his planned renaissance of Worcester City.

  Lancaster's tap roots run deeply into the club he is trying to save from oblivion. He watched them at St George's Lane when he was knee high to his grandfather, who had held a season ticket since the 1940s. He was there with his eldest son, the fourth generation to watch Worcester City, when they kicked Coventry City out of the FA Cup in 2014.

  To this day, his place is on the terraces with the fans.

  'I'm no Ryan Reynolds,' he says of the tinsel town American millionaire, who poured in millions to rouse Welsh sleeping giant Wrexham.

  'But from where we were, when I came in, the only way is up; to be honest, you couldn't go any lower with the finances and the football.'

  OK, the successful entrepreneur turns over millions in his business, but, on the face of it, Lancaster embodies the kind of modest understatement and plain speaking that I missed in the years spent reporting around the world far from my Worcestershire home.

  'Last season [2022/23], bearing in mind we were at the lowest of the low, we were still getting crowds of 400 and 500 – the average gate in that league is 40 or 50 – I said to the manager in the summer if you can get 500 to watch that shit, imagine how many will come if we become decent!' says Lancaster with a smile. You can't say it plainer than that.

In his professional life, Lancaster has vast experience of spinning adversity into gold with his steady, cautious and professional management style.

His own business was born of being left jobless, at the age of 23, by an insurance company in Worcester. He went back to his family home in Fernhill Heath to lick his wounds.

'I sat in the garden for a while. Then, I had a lightbulb moment, ran inside, grabbed a pen and started to scribble,' he says.

Lancaster dashed off a business plan for his own commercial insurance brokerage. It was born in his mother's spare room and raised in Worcester.

'The first day, I had a whip round for a computer, desk and chair and that was me open for business.'

All this in one day. It proved a long, long, wait for many months for people to sign up for Lancaster's commercial insurance brokerage offering. Eventually, the first job arrived: a contract to insure a commercial building in Stoke-on-Trent.

'When I got the cheque, I wanted to frame it, but I needed the money!' says Lancaster.

More than 23 years later, Lancaster doesn't need the money so much, as he turns over more than £30 million with revenue growing by around 10 per cent a year over the last couple of years. He is a registered Lloyds broker and insures everything from tankers taking their chances against Indian Ocean pirates; to hotels on the island of Cape Verde, off the coast of West Africa; right down to the tools of a lone landscape gardener.

His company, SJL Insurance Services, is based in the historic Kays building in the Tything, which runs through the heart of the city. It does plenty of business with security and mining companies in Africa and Asia. These days, he has more than 100,000 customers.

Despite this success, Lancaster maintains the caution and shrewdness of a born insurance man. After all, the Kays building, in which he operates, is a monument to how fast change can wipe a 117-year-old business off the face of the earth.

Kays catalogues were colourful, glossy and packed with pictures of clothes that people wanted to be seen in.

Every home, including mine, had one back in the day. You could flick through on a Sunday afternoon, choose your family's clothes, fill in the form at the back of the catalogue and send it off with a cheque. (For the youngsters, a cheque was a piece of paper, bearing your signature, that could be used as money.) A parcel would arrive at your house, a day or two later.

The rise of the credit card and shopping online killed Kays stone dead.

'I think the scary thing about that is ... I give myself peace of mind, touch wood, that insurance has been around for hundreds of years from Lloyds of London, 'til now, and people will always need insurance,' says Lancaster. But you look at other industries and they have got fantastic businesses, you know, Nokia with their phones and Kodak with their films. And then almost, through no fault of their own, the world changes and they no longer have a business. People don't buy camera rolls [of film] anymore. Great business one day and the next day it is gone. All you can do is move with the times the best you can, but it is crazy.'

Back to the even crazier world of non-League football. In many ways, Lancaster was in the right place, with the right bank balance, at the right time, as Worcester City teetered on the brink of oblivion in the summer of 2023. At the time he was approached, he was coaching youngsters at the club and, in his early 40s, looked young and fit enough to cut a dash down the wing.

Many fans were content to moan in the pubs about the dramatic fall of Worcester City. At the very least, Lancaster was prepared to do something about it.

'They had no assets, and they were losing money; they were due to run out of money this year,' he says not long after taking over the reins in the summer of 2023.

Lancaster took up the gauntlet of raising the club from the depths of the ninth tier of the English game. A thankless job at the best of times.

The day of destiny was 24 May 2023. A meeting convened by the Supporters' Trust of around 80 fans and officials in the pavilion of Worcestershire County Cricket Club, in New Road, on the banks of the River Severn.

Steadily and methodically, Lancaster laid out his plans for the club, ahead of a vote. The concerned fans, weary of decline, listened patiently. They may have owned the club, but didn't have two pennies to rub together.

Club historian Julian Pugh was one of the fans at New Road.

'I think because Simon was involved with the club already, knew some of the supporters, and was coaching one of the youth teams, it wasn't as if somebody had just appeared out of nowhere, some wealthy guy whom nobody knew anything about making all kind of loud claims that he was going to transform the football club,' says Pugh.

'His approach was a little bit humbler than that ... I think that people felt like, "yeah, this is the right thing to do". He happened at the right time because the club was sinking fast, there was no doubt about that. If Simon hadn't intervened, we would not be talking today, would we?'

Another, more cynical fan, who asked not to be named, said with a laugh: 'The good thing is he is from Fernhill Heath, so he can't run away!'

Also in the audience that night was journalist Marcello Cossali-Francis, who was covering the story for the *Worcester News*.

'That evening was very much Simon Lancaster is the saviour, fair to say, and so far, while everything is good, everyone is like "this is great, this is what we are after – if the football can turn around very quickly",' he recalls.

'That day was about we need to get Simon in because he is going to pump money in and we haven't got any of it and the WFA [Worcestershire Football Association] is not giving anything to help us out.'

Yet, it was not as simple as it sounded as Lancaster wound up his presentation of a plan to revive Worcester City.

With the stall set out, the fans, in Lancaster's words, interrogated him for two hours.

'They needed to hand over to someone who could put some cash in, but not only that it was also a bit of a rudderless ship really, it needed some guidance, some leadership and some drive and some energy.'

The vote went 76-1. With this, the fans handed Lancaster 51 per cent of the club and control, a move finalised by lawyers in January 2024.

'I don't know why I couldn't convince that one person!' quips Lancaster with a smile weeks later.

'I agreed to a six-figure sum, a year, for the first three years. They sold St George's Lane years ago and the money has gone over the last 10 to 15 years. It is more about underwriting the losses. About £3m to £2m went on debts, that left a million which has been burned in running the club in the last 15 years. Accountants told the board the club was due to run out of money the following season. It needed to get to that point for me to come in, I suppose.'

There is no doubt, unlike many owners in the professional game, Lancaster is a football man, first and foremost, as well as a rich man. Refreshingly, in the era of detached egomaniacs running our game, he wears his eminence lightly.

'I think he is a genuine guy; he has got all the right intentions. He has not come in to make a quick buck and develop houses and all that stuff.

'There is none of that. He is there to help out, prop it up and give it an immediate future really, he is a self-made man who has created his business. He doesn't really flaunt it to people,' says Dave Wood, a board member and supporter of Worcester City since the 1970s, whom you will see selling tickets on the gate most Saturdays.

At home matches and pretty much all of the away games, Lancaster stands and watches with everyone else, always ready for a chat about the game, or a player. He holds solid views on grassroots football and the dangers of the big money game.

'The gulf is getting wider ... the change in the last decade is obscene. The transfer fees? What did Chelsea spend last season ... £600 million? It is just mental!'

I ask him if he fears for the English grassroots game.

'I do because that gulf is getting so wide and you wonder how it is going to end. Stretch anything like that and it is going to snap at some point, it is just crazy.

'You have got the Saudis putting money in right now, you have got the Americans; as long as there is money coming in at the top level, I just don't see how it is going to end really.

'I think it is a shame because it is the people's game, and they are being priced out of it. It is just a shame that families are finding it too expensive to support these teams really.'

Weeks after the May takeover, Lancaster had taken to the task with a will. He brought in a commercial manager, the only full-time employee at the club, Ryan Molloy, the son of former Worcester City striker Paul Molloy, who played 124 games for the club in the 1990s. He helped sign 15 club sponsors. This was double the number from the season before. Some feat for a club mired in the basement of semi-professional football and not exactly a big draw.

One of these sponsors is Worcester City fan Tim Evans, who owns a toyshop in Broad Street in the city centre, just a hop, skip and a jump from the Paul Pry pub where the club was founded in 1902. He started off his thriving games and jigsaws business at the old Market Hall in the Shambles, 30 years ago, and moved it to Broad Street 20 years ago.

Evans sponsors Worcester City to the tune of £1,500 a season. He admits the new season brought change.

'This year, I am treated like a proper sponsor. Ringing me up: "Tim, what can we do for you?" Last year, I put my board up at the side of the pitch and gave them £500 and that was it. This year, I gave them £1,500, but I didn't really expect much more for it. I thought, we are going to a different level, I will help them on their journey. This year, I got two tickets for the Raiders game; we also had our own game to sponsor!' he says in a coffee shop in Broad Street a few doors away from his shop.

'I just want to help them on their journey. It is not what I get out of it, I just want Worcester City to do well. I get so much enjoyment going to the games and it is better if you are winning. Now, I enjoyed it last year even though we were dire. It matters and everyone there cares and the pain; you sort of enjoy the pain, as well as the good times.'

What does he think of Lancaster?

'I think he is real. I think what Worcester City has been missing is a young, dynamic businessperson who thinks big. I think we might have that person in him,' Evans replies.

'Lancaster insures oil tankers. That is not just farming out house insurance or car insurance. That is bespoke packages for serious business. He runs a Worcester City youth team, he is a local lad, he has got a business with a big vision and straight away he has come in with commitment.'

In this big vision, Lancaster believes Worcester City's small-beer, ninth-tier status is likely to be its biggest handicap for now.

'For a city the size of Worcester that is pretty low. There are teams in the Premier League with smaller populations than Worcester! We need some promotions quite quickly in the medium term ... but you know how business is. The higher you go, the harder it is going to get, and the more money it is going to cost; so, you've got to be realistic in your goals in that sense,' says Lancaster.

'Medium-term goals are to match rivals Kidderminster Harriers in the National League. When we get to that level, we could be getting 5,000 to 10,000 people watching. People here want to watch sport, but they won't at the level we are at now.'

By far the biggest problem Lancaster faces is that Worcester City may now at least have a few bob in the bank, but don't have a home.

Without their own ground, Worcester City will have no control over their destiny, nor will they have a chance of the millions of pounds of Premier League trickle-down money in grants through the Football Association and the government's Football Foundation.

Lancaster accepts that the hurdle of planning permission – or rather planning objections – are likely to be arduous, expensive and painful.

'As you know, finding somewhere and getting planning permission and actually developing it is easier said than done,' he says.

'Everyone wants it, but no one wants it on their doorstep.'

Even if they do, the growing City of Worcester is fast running out of green spaces, full stop, let alone one with room for a car park and a community centre. On top of that, any development is likely to be expensive, running into millions of pounds.

'We had some prices kicking around. Figures are quite scary. As long as you have got a bit of land, a stand and some changing rooms you can add to that; it will be a staged thing,' he says.

By Christmas 2023, the club would dip its toe into the planning pool, yet again.

For now, Lancaster is fairly sanguine about becoming one of England's newest football club owners. A job of sleepless nights and draining worry that many in football say is tantamount to pinning a target on your back.

At the very least, his attempt to rescue the club has earned the respect of former club chairman and fellow Worcester businessman Anthony Hampson.

'People had an ego trip about the club; it was a sleeping giant, as people said, but it needed to come back to reality and start again. This chap [Lancaster] will be able to do that because it is only a small business to run; it is not a big animal.'

I ask Lancaster, why on earth a hard-headed businessman, like he, is doing this to himself.

'I suppose the first point is the heart; Worcester-born-and-bred, supported the club as a boy, sad to see the state they were in and thought that I could have a go at turning it around really. Outside of that I think it is an enjoyable challenge – I might not say that in five years' time, if I get some flak, if things start going the other way and people start calling for my head; I might feel differently!' he says.

'I've got quite a thick skin; you need it really. For now, everything is complimentary, it's all great. When things go the other way I am sure it will feel a bit different. It won't make me any money and I won't take anything out of it. If you look at the Premier League and the FSGs and people like that, they do it to make money. FSG bought Liverpool for £300m. It's valued at about £4bn, it is an investment they will make money on. At this level, Worcester City is not going to make you money, it is not an investment that is going to give me any return at all.'

Of that, there is no doubt.

Chapter 7

Westfields Woe

IT CERTAINLY wasn't going to be a cakewalk in the 2023/24 season. Worcester City may have had more money and momentum than most, but there were plenty of teams striving to put one over on the promotion favourites.

A rude awakening came on a gorgeous warm August night, at Claines Lane, against raiders from west of the border in Herefordshire.

Westfields, based in the city of Hereford, are minnows even at this lower end of the non-League game.

True, their survival is a labour of love for the dedicated volunteers who run the club, but they have rarely been on the radar of Worcester City, aside from friendlies and reserve games.

Survival as a football club is a tough row to hoe in Hereford. The agricultural county town of Hereford, population just under 62,000, is home to no fewer than four non-League clubs. Hereford FC, the phoenix club which rose from the ashes of FA Cup giant-killers Hereford United and which plays in the National League North; Hereford Pegasus; Hereford Lads Club and Westfields, all three in Worcester City's league.

The competition for fans is fierce in a city more famous as the home of Mappa Mundi, the largest medieval map in existence dating from 1300 and displayed in Hereford Cathedral, than professional football.

If you want professional football, for now, you have to leave Hereford. Among its biggest football exports were Kevin Sheedy to Everton and Jarred Bowen to West Ham.

Hereford FC enjoy the lion's share of support, leaving the rest of the city living off the scraps.

Money is so tight for that plethora of clubs that Hereford Lads Club had to drop out of the Hellenic League at the end of the 2023/24 season. It is one of the oldest clubs in Herefordshire, having been founded in 1925 to help underprivileged boys in the city and began life hosting boxing and gymnastics.

The club statement said it could raise only around half of the money it needed to stay in the Hellenic League.

Westfields also struggle in the shadow of Hereford FC. Its tiny ground is next to two huge cider vats making the famous drink of Hereford, just 100 yards through the trees from Edgar Street where Hereford FC draws gates of nearly 3,000.

Westfields struggle to attract a couple of hundred supporters.

Westfields are also relative newcomers. The club was founded in 1966 by a bunch of friends in the Westfields area of the city who were so impressed by England's 1966 World Cup win that they decided to form their own football team.

Most of the lads were Aston Villa supporters so they chose claret and blue for their strip. Their first friendlies were against the Post Office and the Oxford Arms pub, according to the club's history.

One of the founders was 16-year-old goalkeeper Andy Morris, who is chief executive and secretary to this day.

Morris was on the touchline as Westfields ran out at Claines Lane with little hope of success and kicked off in a glorious pink-sky sunset, in August 2023.

Early in the game, one of the Worcester City strikers tried an ambitious first-time volley from far out. It ended up bouncing harmlessly halfway up the bank behind the goal.

'Watches too much television,' said the bloke standing next to me, shaking his head.

'Could have taken a touch!'

Overall, the crowd were pretty quiet at Claines Lane, this early in the season. It was as if they weren't quite sure that this team was the real deal. There were a few angry bellows over stray passes and poor refereeing decisions; mostly subdued as an autumnal nip in the air descended upon the ground.

Despite this there was a roar, almost with relief, as Worcester City took the lead in the first half. A free kick from the right found the fleet-footed, unmarked, Kirk Layton at the far post, who volleyed it in from a couple of yards for his second goal in four games.

Two minutes after half-time and Westfields were level, against the run of play. There was a rapid break to the right of the goal and the striker tried a low shot towards the bottom corner. Worcester City keeper Isaac Parry spread himself and managed to side-foot the shot away, but only into the path of Dan Stoneman, who rifled his shot in before the keeper could recover.

Minutes later, the Westfields keeper made two last-ditch saves to keep his side in it.

Worcester City then hit the post and the ball bounced clear. It seemed it was only a matter of time before Westfields succumbed in the late-night dew.

In the 57th minute, Worcester City brought on Worcester-born Jamie Insall, recently returned from playing in Scotland for Hibernian and East Fife, in a bid to give more options in attack. A defender floored him within minutes with a rough tackle to the knee.

Welcome home, Jamie.

A moment that turned the game came deep into the second half. The Westfields right-back barged over Worcester City's hard-working winger Liam Lockett on the left. Lockett took the free kick and floated a perfect curling ball over to the crowd of players on the right-hand side of the penalty area.

A Worcester City player headed the ball like a bullet into the bottom left-hand corner.

The City players celebrated and ran back up the field. Meanwhile, there was a yellow-shirted Westfield defender lying on the floor. The referee seemed to take an age before running over to the defender, disallowing the goal and awarding a free kick the other way.

I was standing right behind the goal that night. I didn't see anything wrong with it. The Westfields players didn't seem to have a problem.

'Rubbish ref! What was wrong with that?' bellowed a bearded guy behind the goal. 'Can anyone tell me what was wrong with that?'

The referee ruled that Calvin Dinsley had fouled the defender, but it also seemed that he went down after the ball went into the net.

With the wonder of Worcester City TV, I have played the disallowed goal over and over. Still can't see anything wrong. Where is VAR when you need it?

Minutes later, when a shot from afar was first deflected and then touched on to the bar by the keeper it seemed the night was with Westfields. Another fingertip save and the rebound volleyed agonisingly across the face of goal by Insall. Followed by yet another point-blank reflex save.

Then the moment Worcester City fans feared. It was four minutes into injury time. Steve Davies was in possession on the left of the Worcester City penalty area, going nowhere. He just swung his right boot and the ball looped over the keeper and nestled into the bottom right-hand corner of the net.

Pandemonium, the Westfields players ran to hug their ten supporters standing behind the goal. It was a fluke, no doubt about that, but a glorious one.

There was another desperate Worcester City breakaway and then the final whistle.

'Can anyone tell me what was wrong with that goal?' said one of the elder statesmen of the terraces on the way out of the ground. No answer from a fairly sullen crowd leaving Claines Lane on what should have been a night of victory and three points.

'Can anyone tell me how we didn't win 5-1?' said another.

The luck of the game that keeps us coming back week in week out, was the answer.

But on this night, nobody wanted to hear it.

There were even mutterings about whether this was going to be a glory season or not if they can't beat a run-of-the-mill team like Westfields. A fleeting, yet sobering, thought.

No matter, a week later there was a good omen hanging in the skies over Claines Lane ahead of the next home game I managed to get to on 5 September.

A beautiful, orange, full, harvest moon – a sight that always makes me smile. I have seen it many times over Africa, but it never looks as good as when it looms over the harvested fields of Worcestershire, a heart-warming sight. The Anglo Saxons called it the hunter's moon because it reminded them it was time to slaughter animals and prepare meat for the long, dark, winter months. Others call it the blood moon – maybe blood orange – and it inspired poets, a Neil Young album and a computer game.

On this night, Worcester City needed all the good omens they could get as they were out to convince supporters that their season was back on track.

The loss against Westfields was a bit of a rude awakening, albeit unlucky.

Now another bunch of rivals from down the road hove into view – a rejuvenated Pershore Town.

One of the few benefits of Worcester City's tumble down the leagues is that it means more games against lesser, nearer teams, which help swell the gate.

A crowd of 912 turned up for the game. There was a lot of good-natured chat and handshakes behind the goal with talk of how their respective clubs were progressing. Non-League football at its best.

Pershore Town are no walkover. A couple of years earlier I watched Pershore Town beat Worcester City in the final of the Worcestershire Senior Cup at Bromsgrove. Just 20 years earlier, you could have hardly imagined the two clubs on the same pitch.

Under the harvest moon, Pershore Town ran out in their all-red strip and took to attack down the flanks. The highlight of this opening assault was the visitors' long throw specialist who launched the ball from the left touchline to the six-yard box.

'I couldn't kick it that far, never mind throw it,' said the bloke standing next to me.

A few minutes later a desperate clearance bounced on top of the high fence at the side of the ground and disappeared on to the dark Droitwich Road running alongside the ground.

'I'll get that on the way home!' said the wag on my left.

Someone who had no problem finding the ball was Worcester City's two-footed winger Liam Lockett. In the 40th minute, he opened the scoring thanks to a delightful through ball by right-back Logan Stoddard. Lockett slalomed effortlessly past two

Pershore defenders and smacked the ball crisply into the corner of the net. It was his fourth goal in ten games.

'Yes, Locko!' shouted the home fans with fists in the air.

Lockett dealt the killer blow on the stroke of half-time. Worcester City won the ball on the left and after a couple of short passes, Kyle Belmonte held the ball up on the edge of the area before feeding an inch-perfect through ball to Lockett, who chipped it over the advancing keeper.

The goal was so close to half-time a lot of the fans missed it as they queued up in the club for pies and beer.

'At least I heard it,' said one.

Lockett should have completed his hat-trick a couple of minutes into the second half when the Pershore keeper parried a blistering shot from the right into his path. He fluffed the simple task of tapping home the rebound and put his hands on his head.

Pacy winger Izak Reid could have also made it three late into the game, when he rounded the goalkeeper and missed narrowly from a tight angle.

Belmonte then missed a sitter of a free header from about six yards out. Clearly, he closed his eyes.

'Also, he doesn't want to mess up his hair!' said an elder behind the goal.

In the dying seconds, Belmonte had one last chance to make it 3-0 when he latched on to a long ball out of midfield, but he blasted well over from about ten yards.

So, Worcester City had to settle for 2-0 and were applauded off the field.

Maybe the season was on track after all, and Worcester City could wish for the harvest moon as well as play football under it. Their long-term survival depended upon it.

Chapter 8

Eighty Quid a Week?

PICTURE THIS, Gary Lineker scores against West Germany in the World Cup semi-final in Turin in 1990. In 1997, Lineker turns out for Bromsgrove Sporting against Redditch United in the Southern League.

Never happen?

Well, a very similar scenario played out at Worcester City, in 1969, in the wonderful, chaotic, world of non-League football.

The Gary Lineker of his day was Gerry Hitchens, an elegant striker who scored for England against Brazil in the World Cup quarter-final in Valparaiso, in Chile, in 1962. On that day, he played alongside a golden England generation in waiting: Bobby Moore, Bobby Charlton, Jimmy Greaves and Johnny Haynes.

Just over seven years later, Hitchens, fresh from the cultured Serie A in Italy, ran out at St George's Lane in the blue-and-white stripes of Worcester City against Bath City on a cold Monday night in November 1969.

Nick Banks was there to see this remarkable debut in deepest, coldest Worcestershire. These days, Banks is a fit six-footer who can walk from the Droitwich Road to the High Street without even breathing heavily.

In 1969, he was 11 years old and walked the half a mile from his home in Landsdowne Road, with a group of elders from the neighbourhood.

'It was a great atmosphere, and it was clear a lot of people had come down on the night just to see Gerry Hitchens,' he recalls.

'A bloke standing in front of me turned round and says: "Eighty bloody quid a week they're paying him! Bloody ridiculous – you can't pay a footballer that!" The rest of us just couldn't believe we were watching a player of that quality at St George's Lane.'

At this point in his career, quality ran through Hitchens like letters in a stick of rock. He rode tackles with ease after years of suffering rough treatment in Italy, and turned the non-League defenders with little effort. He was still only 35 and arguably in his prime with vast experience; he was certainly too classy for the likes of Bath City.

Hitchens possessed rare talent and drive. He was born in Rawnsley, Staffordshire and forged in the depths of the nearby coal mines of Highley, in Shropshire.

Square-jawed, blond and handsome; Hitchens would have made a fortune from his image if he had been born in 1994, instead of 1934.

Yet, it took him a few years to make his mark in Worcestershire, let alone anywhere else. Hitchens started his playing days on the bottom rung of Sunday football with Highley Miners' Welfare, alongside his fellow cutters of coal.

It was not until the miners got to a County Cup final in 1954 – just eight years before his goal against Brazil at the World Cup in Chile – that Hitchens got his break. A scout for Kidderminster Harriers, a Southern League side just down the road, spotted him.

Kidderminster signed Hitchens for the following season with a promise of first-team football. It was to prove another struggle for Hitchens as he had to campaign hard for the mere 14 games he played for Kidderminster Harriers. In those days, good things took time.

My father, journalist Tony Bishop, reported on one of those games for the *Kidderminster Shuttle*. He was always proud to tell me, years later, that he wrote that Hitchens would one day play for England.

This prediction was unlikely to come true if Hitchens stayed much longer at Kidderminster Harriers.

Luckily for Hitchens, the club sold him to Cardiff City, for £2,000 in January 1955, where his goalscoring took off. The miner-turned-striker scored 57 goals in 108 games for the Welsh side.

FA Cup winners Aston Villa, in need of a dashing new striker, took note of the goals flying in for Cardiff City.

In December 1957, Villa paid £29,000 for Hitchens who formed a deadly partnership with Peter McParland, also destined to play for Worcester City. He banged in 96 goals in four seasons.

This form also earned an England call-up, at the age of 26, against Mexico in May 1961. Hitchens scored after only 90 seconds in an 8-0 rout. He was to score five goals in seven appearances in an England career which was to be cut cruelly short.

On one of his golden afternoons, Hitchens scored two as England beat Italy 3-2 in Rome.

This stellar performance caught the eye of Inter Milan, who paid £107,000 for him; you could buy a whole team and a street full of houses for that kind of money back then.

The move was a gift for newspaper headline writers: 'From the mine to Milan'.

Hitchens said he wanted to play in different places against different teams; he had made it out of the pit and now he wanted to see how far he could go.

In those days, foreign travel for most English people, never mind footballers, was rare; exchange controls were a problem for a start.

You could count the number of English footballers playing in Europe on two hands.

They included Welsh giant John Charles – the Lion of Turin – who played for Juventus and also graced the St George's Lane turf while playing for Hereford United later in his career. Banks recalls seeing Charles pick the ball up with one hand to deliver long throws into the penalty box long before the tactic was the norm.

An Englishman alone at training, in Milan, Hitchens didn't find it easy to fit in.

'Inter's policy of keeping players together a few days in advance of each match proved particularly difficult for the Englishman. Possessing little Italian, at least in the beginning, the containment policy effectively left Hitchens isolated. Luckily, he found a kindred spirit in fellow Englishman Jimmy Greaves, then playing for bitter rivals AC Milan. The two would sneak out of training camps for drinks at a local Milanese train station. Remarkably, neither was ever caught,' wrote the Football Times website in May 2019.

With the Inter fans he was a hit. As ever, the Italian journalists always came up with grand names for the fans' favourites. Writers called Hitchens '*Il Cannone*' (the cannon) and the priceless moniker '*Il Principe del Gioco del Calcio*' (The Prince of Football). Not bad for a humble Highley coal miner.

Hitchens played in Italy for eight years, believed to be the longest stint abroad by an English player in the professional era. He gradually adapted to life in Italy and began to enjoy the rich technicolour of the Dolce Vita and signed for three more Italian clubs: Torino, Atalanta and Cagliari.

His international career was taking off too. For a man who struggled to break into the Kidderminster Harriers team, a call-up to play for England in the 1962 World Cup in Chile must have caused him to pinch himself. Legend has it that he took 19 Italian designer suits with him.

He scored against Brazil in the defeat in the quarter-final, which proved to be his baffling swansong, bearing in mind he was at the height of his powers.

England manager Sir Alf Ramsey made it clear, when he took over the job in the build-up to the 1966 victory, that no foreign-based players would be considered. A world before satellite TV, world rankings and common sense.

This effectively isolated Hitchens from international football. After a short stint in Sicily with Cagliari he returned home, not to the top flight, but to Worcester City of the Southern League to play the likes of Margate, Romford and Poole.

Many supporters thought Hitchens was slightly over the hill, but undoubtedly, he was a Rolls-Royce of a striker in a Southern League used to second-hand Ford Consuls.

Even this move took time, according to reports – it was finalised only in the November when Cagliari made it clear they didn't require a fee.

For the debut of Hitchens, against Bath City on a Monday night, the crowd at St George's Lane was 3,037 – nearly three times the attendance for the previous league game. The crowd included the wide-eyed 11-year-old Banks, from Landsdowne Road.

Banks played for Worcester City reserves when he grew up and made a name for himself in the city's sports fraternity. He says seeing Hitchens inspired him.

'At the end of the game our next-door neighbour and his friends went to the pub, and I walked home alone in the dark of a November night. I was 11, no one said a word – different times!'

Hitchens played for Worcester City until 1971, before a transfer to Merthyr. He scored 34 goals in 72 games for the club.

Sadly, the former England maestro lived out the rest of his days in relative obscurity. He died during a charity football match in Wales in 1983, aged just 48.

Banks, who ran a highly successful record store in the market hall in the Shambles in Worcester, saw many big names at St George's Lane in his decades as both a player and supporter.

One day he watched a game with his mate at St George's Lane next to one of the musicians who sang on many of his favourite records.

'I looked behind and I saw Robert Plant, in a trench coat, on the terraces with the fans. He often used to come to watch games,' he says. Plant, a Wolverhampton Wanderers fan and man of the Midlands who often went to watch at Worcester and Kidderminster.

'My mate, a big Led Zeppelin fan says: "Oh God. I've got to run home." He ran off home to St John's, which is a fair way away. He came back 45 minutes later with his arms full of his entire Led Zeppelin record collection.'

The fan approached Plant at the back of the terrace, who duly signed each album cover. When he'd finished Plant turned to the fan with his arms full of albums.

'Why do you bring your records to a football match?'

The club attracted a score of household names to St George's Lane in the gathering post-war prosperity in Worcester including England international and FA Cup winner Norman Deeley, Welsh international Roy Paul and FA Cup winner McParland to name just a few. In the days of the maximum wage in the top flight the players could earn as much playing for Worcester as they could playing for a First Division club.

These were the years when people were hungry for football after the misery and of the war years and non-League clubs were keen to kick-start operations to get the crowds back.

Worcester City always had big ambitions but lacked the deep pockets to back them up and went bump a few times as a result.

In 1950, bankruptcy was knocking on the door. The club sacked its manager Jack Vinall to save money and asked the players to take a pay cut.

'Worcester's worries can be traced to the years immediately following the war when the club attempted to do too much and incurred too much expenditure out of keeping for a club in their position,' reported the *Sports Argus* on 7 October 1950. To add insult to injury, Worcester City's application to join the Football League received just one vote at the end of a miserable campaign.

It had been a season of huge crowds. There were 8,982 at St George's Lane for a first round FA Cup game against Hartlepool; 4,249 saw City draw 0-0 with Kidderminster Harriers in the Worcestershire Senior Cup first round and 3,404 saw City beat Brierley Hill 2-1 in the final.

But the big wage bill meant the losses piled up.

By the end of the season the club had lost £1,745 1s and 4d – enough to pay Gerry Hitchens for nearly 22 weeks.

'City always spent more money than they earned,' chuckled supporter Gerald Boddy, who was a regular on the St George's Lane terraces at the time.

They were also often hard up. I remember hearing an interview with City legend Harry Knowles on BBC Radio Hereford and Worcester, in 2013, recalling how once the club was so short of money it paid the players in chickens; one or two of the directors were poultry farmers. He said the players expected a plucked chicken, but no, the directors tossed a sack of live chickens into the dressing room who soon escaped and each player had to catch their own wages for the pot.

A 'Save the City' fund was launched and the Supporters' Club chipped in with £800 to ease the club's financial embarrassment.

The Football Association came up with a £5,000 loan and a fund-raising game was staged at St George's Lane starring none other than big-hearted England star Stanley Matthews.

If you can imagine current England stars Jude Bellingham and Harry Kane taking a night off to help raise money for a Southern League club, this was it.

Around 10,520 people squeezed into St George's Lane in May 1951 for the game. It raised £9,211 for the 'Save the City' fund to help the club keep going.

During the game Matthews – King of the dribble – turned a former player for Rangers, by the name of Gordon Mackenzie, inside out several times.

Mackenzie was a serving soldier stationed at nearby Norton Barracks and in frustration he launched a reckless tackle which injured shuffling Stan. The great man was forced to limp off 15 minutes before the end with a bruised foot.

The injury meant Matthews missed two England games including a prestigious international against Argentina. You can only imagine how, these days, there would be newspaper headlines, an FA inquiry and a call for compensation.

Worcester City directors expressed their displeasure by never picking Mackenzie again.

Inexplicably, a year after dancing with bankruptcy, the club was throwing money around yet again the following season hoping that a sprinkle of stardust could win back the crowds.

The newspapers called it 'the great gamble' aimed at putting Worcester on the football map. It was a big, bold, post-war, boast at a time when Worcester and the rest of Britain was still suffering under austerity and rationing.

In came a slew of stars from top-flight football, albeit slightly past their best, of whom most Worcester City fans had merely read about in the newspapers.

In came 33-year-old former Welsh international Danny Winter from Chelsea, where he made 131 appearances, as the captain of Worcester City.

The left-back believed his arrival in Worcester was kismet. Winter fought in the Royal Artillery in the rearguard action at Dunkirk in 1940. The destroyer HMS *Worcester* evacuated

Winter off the beach; when he arrived in England he was put on to a train to Norton Barracks, near Worcester, the home of the Worcestershire Regiment. Just over ten years later he was back in Worcester as a footballer.

Joining Winter was Chelsea centre-forward and leading goalscorer Hugh Billington along with club-mate left back Malcolm Evans. Wing-half Eddie Wilcox, full-back John Flavell, inside-left Norman Allsopp, all moved from West Bromwich Albion.

Ted Duggan, listed at £3,500, came from Queens Park Rangers, inside-forward Peter Donnelly came from Birmingham City and goalkeeper Fred Newman from Blackpool. Newman was an interesting character, according to the official history of Worcester City. His real name was Fritz Neumann and he was a former German prisoner of war along with Manchester City's famed keeper Bert Trautmann. Newman became a great favourite with the Worcester crowd.

Worcester City reaped the rewards through the turnstiles. More than 8,000 saw City beat Merthyr in the first home league game of the season at St George's Lane, The travelling Welshmen must have wondered what was going on!

There were nearly 6,000 for the quarter-final of the Worcestershire Senior Cup against Kidderminster Harriers.

In all, 94,917 people paid to watch football at St George's Lane with and average gate of 4,520 in the 1951/52 season.

Worcester City may have been pulling in the crowds, but were no nearer to the Football League. At the end of the season, the club yet again applied for election to the Football League; this time they received three votes.

'I'm no Ryan Reynolds!' Simon Lancaster the quiet millionaire trying to save Worcester City.

Teenager Tommy Skuse scores the first goal against Liverpool at St George's Lane on 15 January 1959.

Worcester City fans invade the pitch to celebrate victory over Liverpool.

Worcester City thrash Millwall 5-2 in the third round of the FA Cup at St George's Lane.

Worcester City captain and former Welsh international Roy Paul is mobbed as fans invade the pitch after beating Liverpool 2-1.

Andy and Andy – Bullingham (left) and Pountney – the owners of Stourbridge FC. (Photo: John Bray)

Dave Boddy (left) and Anthony Hampson, the Worcester City chairman when St George's Lane was sold to make way for housing.

The glory team – Worcester City win the Southern League Premier division in 1979.

Malcolm Allison in his element with fedora in hand before the crowds.

John Barton – Worcester City's right-back who broke the club's transfer record, in 1978, by signing for Everton for £27,500.

Former professional, part-time Worcester City winger and full-time electrician Izak Reid.

Worcester City score in the first leg of the FA Vase semi final at Sixways in Worcester in the 2023/24 season.

Worcester City's Kirk Layton and Great Wakering Rovers player Callum Boylan tussle for the ball in the semi-final at Sixways.

A teenage Liam McDonald, the first graduate of Worcester City's short lived youth training scheme who now manages Stourbridge.

Worcester City striker Kyle Belmonte scores against Cinderford.

Success at Pershore Town as promoted Worcester City lift the league title at the end of the 2023/24 season. Jamie Insall is carried off shoulder high in his last game before retirement.

Creative midfielder Jamie Insall of Worcester City.

Worcester City legend Lionel Martin in his prime.

Farewell – a ticket for the last game at St George's Lane in 2013, versus Chester City.

St George's Lane once held 17,000 spectators – now it is a housing estate.

The sponsor – toy shop owner Tim Evans, who puts money into Worcester City every season.

All-time top goalscorer John Inglis, who scored 189 goals in 324 games for Worcester City between 1970 and 1976 when a cruel head injury cut short his career.

Peter Fryar – the patriarch of Kidderminster Harriers. (Photo: John Bray)

The biggest crowd ever at St George's Lane – 17,000 v Sheffield United in 1959.

Chapter 9

The Good Old Days.
Not if You Were Black

WE SOMETIMES look back at non-League football with
slightly rose-tinted glasses. More innocent times, more prosperous
times, you name it. Yet the following incident was one of many
that showed the ugly underbelly of the beautiful semi-professional
game.

It happened in a flash and was as ugly as it sounds.

We were in moist Oswestry, a green market town in the
Welsh Marches famous for cows and the First World War poet
Wilfred Owen.

To be fair, it is a bit of a one-horse town. On this Saturday, in
April 1979, it was also a one racist town as Oswestry Town took
on Stourbridge in the Southern League.

Stourbridge striker Tony Cunningham, born in Kingston,
Jamaica, bred in Wolverhampton, picked up the ball on the left a
few yards from where I stood near the rail around the pitch. He
was always great to watch when he was bursting forward in the
red-and-white stripes of Stourbridge.

The month before he had scored two against Worcester City
at St George's Lane to set up a shock 2-1 win in the Worcestershire
Senior Cup semi-final.

Cunningham was 6ft 2in, with a rare turn of speed for a tall
lanky guy and a subtle drop of the shoulder that could fox most
Southern League defenders.

When he went up for the ball, his knees and elbows looked
after him. Woe betide a defender who thought they could beat
him in the air.

In his last season at Stourbridge, he also developed a shot like a cannonball which netted him 17 league goals.

I was 16 years old, full of life and football. It was spring and I was keen to see 21-year-old Cunningham play one of his last games for Stourbridge, before a £15,000 move to the professional game with Lincoln City. You could buy a couple of non-League teams for that kind of money then.

That is why I had badgered my father to drive us many miles to Oswestry Town on that hopeful spring day. He reported on the game in the tin main stand for his paper, the *Wolverhampton Express and Star* , while I found a vantage point on the opposite side of the ground on the grassy bank.

Cunningham was soon in the thick of it. As he darted forward on the left, Cunningham lost the ball to a bone-crunching challenge. Frustrated, he chased back and dived in with a flying, sliding tackle.

In my mind's eye, I can still see the sword slash of mud made by his right boot on the wet grass. OK, these days it would have been a yellow card, at least. In the game of the 1970s it was merely a robust challenge. You would see outrageous tackles of that nature every few minutes.

Cunningham's opposite number crashed to the turf and the ball bounced out into the hands of a grey-haired man standing next to me in car coat and wire-rimmed glasses. He looked like your grandad fresh from the fireside, who would be home in time for tea.

'You dirty black bastard!' he shouted and threw the ball back overarm, with venom, at Cunningham.

Cunningham trapped the ball with his chest and volleyed it back into the face of the racist grandad.

The old man moved forward as if to throw a punch, then thought better of it. Cunningham stood, stock still, next to the touchline staring the man in the eye. Defiant. The referee came over and asked Cunningham what had happened.

'Fair enough, play on,' said the slightly enlightened, for his day, man with a whistle.

I looked at the old racist on the touchline. In those days, teenagers didn't question their elders. In my heart, I felt nothing but contempt. At least, the grandad looked a little shame-faced as I stared and so he should have been.

These days I would have called him out, with a scowl. Told him to get stuffed at the very least; told him that it was wrong to treat another human being in that way and he should be ashamed.

It is no excuse, but in those days we from conservative homes were tongue-tied when it came to criticising our elders.

Fast forward 50 years and more than half of the Stourbridge team is of colour; so are many of their fans.

Sickening racism may lurk under the surface, in English life as a whole, but at least the attempts to stamp it out on the football pitch have stepped up admirably.

At Bromsgrove Sporting on Boxing Day 2023, a racist comment, similar to that of Oswestry in 1979, came over the fence from a supporter. The referee stopped the game, versus Stourbridge, for ten minutes and threatened to take the players off.

At another game at Stratford Town against Stourbridge a supporter sang out: 'Get your tits out for the lads,' when one of the game's many young female physiotherapists ran on to tend to an injury.

Straight away, the referee threatened to take the players off the field if there was not an apology and agreement to desist.

In the 2023/24 season, Stourbridge were cautioned, this time for an incident at a home game. The Express and Star reported on 22 March 2024: 'The alleged incident, which was reported to match officials, concerned "improper" and "indecent" comments and chants directed towards a female member of staff for the opposition, which also made reference to gender.'

The Glassboys have been fined, formally warned and will face further sanction and stiffer punishment from the FA in future if such discriminatory comments and chants are made again.

Stourbridge, who will also need to implement an action plan to address the matter, say they 'deplore' the comments and are extremely 'disappointed' by a small number of home followers.

Sadly, it was nothing, in the last century, to hear a supporter call a player a woman during a game. When I told my strident mother over the tea table, she questioned how someone, in their right mind, could try to turn a compliment into an insult.

Any young woman on the terraces at a game back then could be called, sneeringly, a 'team bike' in plain hearing of the entire terrace.

When it came to racism, black players of the day were as courageous as they were rare in non-League football. It was a nasty little world for them in the 1970s and 1980s. I remember thinking that they must have really loved football to put up with the level of racist abuse every week.

People laughed when a drunken idiot in the main stand at Stourbridge hurled abuse when a black player stripped off to come on as substitute for one of the teams from down south. We used to call the idiot 'The Duke' because he was always drinking in The Duke William a short walk from the ground.

'That's not nice,' said an old man to his friend next to me on the terrace, with at least a tone of sadness in his voice.

No, it bloody wasn't, it was degrading for all of us; but then again, there was little understanding of, or sanction against, this kind of poison then.

In those days many, even intelligent and educated people on the terraces, used to see black players as 'them' coming into 'our' game. Nonsense. Even then, many of the black players playing were born and bred in Britain; black people had lived and worked in the country for hundreds of years.

I admired those pioneering black footballers who bore so much with dignity, stoicism and defiant humour.

At Worcester City there was Compton Edwards. He learned his trade as a swift and deadly winger amid the scything tackles of Sunday football in Birmingham.

Edwards signed from Cinderford Town and banged in 32 goals in 56 games for Worcester City. Legend has it, someone questioned whether he was English. So, for a number of games, Edwards took to running out on to the field wearing a city gent-style bowler hat and carrying an umbrella.

To this day, Worcester City keeps that bowler in pride of place on the wall of the boardroom at Claines Lane.

Yet, it was Cunningham, in the red-and-white stripes of Stourbridge, who inspired me most with his stoicism on the pitch and his quiet zeal off it.

I once overheard heard him talking to a bunch of friends, on the touchline, after a game at Stourbridge. I was struck by how a man who could wreak so much havoc on the pitch was so polite, erudite and softly spoken off it. A true gentleman.

Every Saturday, Cunningham girded his loins against vicious tackles and a barrage of insults from opposition players and supporters alike.

I know it sounds a bit embarrassing, for a man in his sixties, but he was one of my first footballing heroes.

Even our own supporters used to get on his back, calling him 'Snowflake' and 'Kunta Kinte'. They were some of the milder insults.

They used to say when he bruised, he turned white – ha ha ha, they used to laugh. These were the days, after all, when the neo-Nazi National Front marched the high streets of Britain and stood in the 1979 election.

In that season, Cyrille Regis and Laurie Cunningham, two of most cultured and fleet-footed ball artists I have ever seen, were scoring for fun at West Bromwich Albion, just down the road at the Hawthorns.

The beauty on the pitch was often marred by cowardly idiots making monkey noises off it whenever those talented two got the ball. When I was a teenager, I saw fathers teaching their little sons to do it. It made me sick.

Inside football grounds it was common to see a moustachioed muppet with an NF badge on the lapel of his Harrington jacket bellowing abuse at the only black player on the park. They also stood outside football grounds selling the *Bulldog* magazine; they thought young, white, working-class football fans were their constituency that would drive the party to power and glory. Thank heaven they were wrong.

This abuse came with the bullshit theory that black players weren't as committed as white players, and they didn't like the cold weather.

The irony was that Cunningham had grown up and learned his football just down the road in Wolverhampton. His parents arrived from Kingston, Jamaica, where he didn't play football, in the 1960s, when he was seven years old and he grew up supporting Leeds United. He told me more than half a century later, Wolverhampton was home, and he loved it.

Cunningham was a rangy striker who learned his trade in the Wolverhampton Sunday League playing both centre half and centre-forward for Club Lafayette. Decades later he recalled he didn't start any fights but finished a few.

The young striker caught the eye of scouts for Kidderminster Harriers and the Worcestershire club signed him for £14 a week.

Peter Fryar, a former director of Kidderminster Harriers, recalls Cunningham had no transport to get the 16 miles south from Wolverhampton to Worcestershire. Fryar and his wife used to drive him to and from games.

At the end of his first season with the Harriers, Cunningham had done well and scored a few.

At the start of the 1977/78 season, Cunningham went to the new Harriers manager Allan Grundy, who managed Stourbridge in their promotion-winning glory days, to ask for an extra pound a week. It is hard to believe in this day and age, I know. For want of a pound the striker was lost!

According to Fryar, Grundy said no, and Cunningham went to Stourbridge, who could afford that elusive extra pound a week. By today's standards, you could hardly call him mercenary.

At Stourbridge, Cunningham struggled through his first season, but his best days came in the worst of times the following season.

It was the winter of 1978/79. The newspapers called it the Winter of Discontent. It seemed everyone, including my hard-working father, was on strike in the dying days of Jim Callaghan's crumbling Labour government.

Rubbish, run with rats, piled up on the streets of London and there seemed to be picket lines everywhere; soldiers drove fire engines in place of striking firefighters.

The weather was just as miserable as my striking journalist father. It was one of the coldest winters on record with snow and ice ruling our lives for months.

On the football fields of England, the freezing weather took a heavy toll even in the days when six inches of snow, or an inch of water was OK by the referees of the day.

As long as the pitch could take a stud, as they used to say, the game was on.

Not that pitch quality mattered much in non-League football. Worcester City, Kidderminster Harriers and Stourbridge all played on mud heaps with a little bit of grass down the wings pretty much from September to April.

On bad days, pitch preparation meant sweeping the snow off the pitch markings or brushing the worst of the flood water on to the sidelines.

Yet, in 1978/79, matches across the country were frozen or snowed off including quite a few Stourbridge games. Something the club didn't need as it was struggling near the foot of the table.

When Stourbridge games did commence, in the depths of January, the club played Tuesday, Thursday and Saturday for months to try to clear the backlog of fixtures. Imagine the howls of outrage about conditioning and player fatigue in the modern non-League game!

The stage was set for the forceful Cunningham who took to the freezing pitches with a will, developing his career rapidly and slaying racist myths as he went. Black players don't like the cold or lack grit? Rubbish!

It paved the way for Cunningham's transfer from Stourbridge to Lincoln City in 1979. His debut at Sincil Bank was against Barnsley. The late England defender Norman Hunter marked Cunningham in the game; the striker proved too quick and powerful for the former international. Hardman Hunter returned to Lincoln in 1982 – when Cunningham had matured as a professional striker – to buy him for Barnsley for £92,000. More than 40 years later Cunningham told me Hunter said he had been impressed by his performance against him a couple of years before.

The career of Cunningham rose above the racists and proved an inspiring tale for young black footballers. With sheer grit and determination, he forged a career at Newcastle United, Sheffield Wednesday, Manchester City, Blackpool and Bolton Wanderers. Once he played on for Newcastle United with a strapped-up dislocated shoulder.

It is nice to think that all of that racist rubbish is in the dustbin of history. Sadly, think again.

A couple of generations later, Worcester City winger Izak Reid suffered racial abuse when playing an away game in his professional playing days for League Two Morecambe in the League Cup against Millwall in London.

'I thought, we're League Two to your Championship, were not even local, were from up north. So, to have that sort of anger and venom in your words? And that was at Millwall. Yeah, I think I got fouled at the time, so I could hear them saying all the obvious to me, and I remember sitting there and going: wow, that's horrendous like, I'm a nobody in the greatest respects to like, where you're challenging and what you're doing, and it's little Morecambe, and we've come down, for a nice experience, it's quite a big game for us, playing a Championship team, and I'm sat here getting racially abused,' he says with an air of resignation.

'But then I've had it for Morecambe, when I was playing at Accrington Stanley. I've stood on the goalpost with the fans right behind me, racially abusing me, and it's just like: wow; in this day and age?'

You have to argue that non-League grounds are much more civilized and safer places with the zero tolerance to racism and sexism which is taken seriously.

With the sublime can come the ridiculous. I remember one winter's afternoon standing on the terrace behind the goal.

A team from down south had been beaten soundly and one of the supporters behind the goal was having his day at the expense of the visiting goalkeeper, as the final minutes ticked away.

'It's OK keeper they've started up the engine of the bus,' said he.

'We've got some faggots and peas for you before you go!'

The goalkeeper snapped around pointing an accusatory finger at the terraces.

'That is homophobic language!' he said, pointing his right hand angrily towards the terraces. Everyone behind the goal rolled their eyes and threw back their heads.

Anyone in the Black Country will tell you that faggots are a local delicacy that your mother must have served to you at some stage in your life. It is a spiced meatball with chopped liver mixed in and gravy. Obviously, the goalkeeper was oblivious.

There came forth almost comical dispute from the terraces.

'It's food, it's food,' said the man who started it all, using his left hand to depict a bowl of faggots with his right hand dipping in with an imaginary fork.

'Don't be ridiculous. It's a meatball. It is food!' I shouted. I normally wouldn't waste my breath, but this was ludicrous.

'Well, he must watch his mouth!'

Sure enough, but we all ended up shaking our heads.

At the end of the game the goalkeeper ran to the referee and reported the alleged homophobic language. You can only imagine a bowl of faggots and gravy being produced as evidence at a league disciplinary hearing. Thankfully, the referee didn't see fit to report the incident.

Surely such misunderstandings will only negate the good work that is being done to protect our footballers whatever their creed, colour or sexual orientation. That is something of which non-League football can be proud.

Chapter 10

Doomed in Droitwich

THERE ARE peaks and troughs in every club. In the last 40-odd years Worcester City's steady dive to the bottom has been like watching a luxury ocean liner sink beneath the waves.

Many fans believe Worcester City's powers peaked a lifetime ago in 1979, the year the nation elected Margaret Thatcher.

They feel years of storming the Southern League – unbeaten in all games bar one in 1976/77 – and becoming a founder of the Alliance Premier League, in 1979, was the pinnacle.

The brave new APL, the forerunner of the National League, bristled with the strongest semi-professional teams in the land: Yeovil; Altrincham; Barrow; Boston and Barnet. Worcester City went toe to toe with all comers before loyal thousands who followed the side around the country.

In the first season of the APL City had average gates of 1,935 as the club finished third.

Therefore, you can only imagine that sinking feeling for some of the older supporters as they arrived at Droitwich on a cold November night near the end of 2023.

None of the players, nor most of the supporters, were even born in Worcester City's heyday of the 1970s.

It was a return to the scene of a painful memory for many Worcester City supporters on another cold November night the year before.

The City faithful believe the previous season's 3-0 hammering, in the Worcestershire Senior Cup, at the hands of nearby little brothers down the road, Droitwich Spa, was the lowest point in the club's 120-year history. They include the club's historian, Julian Pugh, who has been watching Worcester City since he was a teenager in the late 1970s. He remembers that night of 18 October 2022, clearly and ruefully.

'It was a big game for Droitwich. It was their record crowd. Worcester was in this odd interim period where we had appointed two guys as joint managers, [Keenen Meakin-Richards and Graham Deakin] that nobody had ever heard of. They came and ripped the team apart, brought in loads of players, that nobody had ever heard of, and were quite clearly not interested in playing for Worcester City,' he says.

Pugh recalls all through, a slightly pained smile, as we talk in a clattering coffee shop in the Shambles, just inside the old city walls of Worcester. The street was so-named because it was where butchers plied their trade for centuries; an apt venue for a chat about slaughter.

'Went to Droitwich on a Tuesday night, Worcester were 3-0 down after the first 45 minutes and I thought: this is absolutely appalling!' he says. It stayed that way.

'Losing to a local team and losing comprehensively. If you think, Worcester and Kidderminster Harriers were the two big Worcestershire teams competing; that hasn't happened for 40 years now. Worcester were reduced to competing with Stourport and Droitwich? I think that most people were resigned to accepting the fact that this was awful. It was kind of too awful to get worked up about. We just accepted, we are where we are, we will have to live with it and take it on the chin.'

Someone once wrote, hell was the impossibility of reason. A year on from the 3-0 debacle, reason and the form book expected a rejuvenated Worcester City to destroy Droitwich Spa in revenge.

Surely, Droitwich Spa away in the Senior Cup was going to be different this year?

Worcester City arrived in the backyard of the country cousins on the back of ten straight league wins.

Worcester's hungry forwards had smashed in goals, from every angle, for months. What could possibly go wrong?

Worcester City may play in a league higher than Droitwich Spa, but the hosts were also brimming with confidence.

Fans expected a big away following in Droitwich; at least 500 made the trip from Worcester.

In City's down days, in 2014 and 2015, around 20 supporters was a good away following.

Famously, on a cold night in Southport, for a rearranged FA Trophy tie, seven Worcester City supporters made the journey. Unbelievably, club officials segregated all seven of them on a vast, windswept, terrace. They took a picture to mark the occasion.

A win for Worcester City in Droitwich would also be cathartic in easing the pain on the pitch. Back in 2022, the word inept would have been quite kind about a limp and lacklustre Worcester City in the depths of the doldrums.

At the time, my expectations of Worcester City were very low. The next day I sought out the highlights online simply because I couldn't believe it!

To make matters worse, this was a humiliation in one of Britain's oldest and least significant cups, the Worcestershire Senior Cup, which Worcester City have won a record 28 times.

It may be a nothing cup, but it has always managed to summon up that swell of civic pride across Worcestershire. At the very least, it promised clubs a dash of glamour at the end of another lean season.

For nearly 130 years, the aspiring teams of the county have written headlines in the cup in tense tussles for, what would be called these days on Sky Sports, 'the bragging rights'.

The 130-year-old trophy is a lot grander than the competition itself. It is big, bold and almost sparkles under the floodlights.

Elkington's of Birmingham made it and it cost the Worcestershire Football Association £50. In 1902, Worcester City was valued at a mere £72; to put it in context, my great-grandfather was feeding a family of 13 on a handful of shillings a week.

The family business of Elkington's was the first to patent the electroplating process. It can take pride that one of its creations is still glittering more than a century after it was silver-plated and chucked around muddy Worcestershire fields by sweaty winning teams.

The Senior Cup looks more like a polo trophy, rather than a cup fought for by the muddy working men of Worcestershire.

The footballers of the county have vied for it ever since 1894. Redditch Town beat Oldbury 3-1, to win it for the first time.

In the last century, the finals were contested fiercely before thousands of roaring rival supporters, usually over two legs. In the 1960s and 1970s, up to 5,000 would turn up for finals and semi-finals.

I have watched and reported on scores of Worcestershire Senior Cup games over the last 50 years and more often than not they were blood-and-thunder encounters. After all, in more parochial times for football, it was ours and dripped with inter-community rivalry.

Let's face it, there wasn't that much else to do in Kidderminster, Stourbridge or Worcester on a Monday night, when the cup games were usually played!

I can still see the blue stripes on the back of the muddy, steaming, Worcester City captain Lionel Martin, a hard-as-nails former professional with Aston Villa, who looked like he had been carved from granite.

In my mind's eye, I can picture him in triumph on the shoulders of his players on the Aggborough turf. He held the silver cup high over his head at the end of a hard-fought 1-0 victory away at Kidderminster Harriers, in the spring of 1978, before 1,134 paying customers, including me. A 3-2 victory in the two-legged final thanks to a rare goal from towering centre-half Kevin Tudor.

On that spring night, hundreds of travelling City supporters went wild as if they had won the FA Cup. That is how much it meant, then, in a string of full-blooded finals that people looked forward to.

The following year, Kidderminster Harriers beat Stourbridge 4-3 over two legs, thanks to an own goal, to lift the trophy. Harriers captain John Chambers, in his sweat-drenched red shirt, did the honours with the trophy that night high in the stands; grabbing it with one hand and clenching his other fist like a boxer.

The combative former Villa trainee Chambers was one of the larger-than-life characters of non-League football in Worcestershire. He played for City, Harriers and Stourbridge and ended up managing at Aggborough and Amblecote.

'I love it!' I heard him say, through a wide grin, to the clicking photographer from the *Kidderminster Times*. That was him.

In 1981, on a dark and muddy night, Chambers was on the losing side and didn't love it.

Stourbridge won the two-legged final with a superb snap volley by Glen Hughes and a clever back-heel into the bottom corner by Brendan Drummond. The latter was a deft touch that the commentators would have raved about in the Premier League era. Then, we just thought, 'Why didn't he turn and kick it properly?'

In cup games like this Kidderminster Harriers wore their sponsored shirts, with the letters IKE, long before it was allowed in the professional game.

These shirts were paid for by Bet with Ike, a Kidderminster bookie who had taken bets in the town for generations.

Harriers always seemed to lose in the cup when they wore those bright red IKE shirts. The grammar-school boys in the home crowd used to say the letters stood for Ignominious Kidderminster Exit.

So it was on that warm spring night. Stourbridge's black-bearded captain Roger Minton, a hard-working right-back formerly with West Bromwich Albion, held the glistening cup high over his head with arms outstretched and a piratical cackle of joy.

More than 40 years on, I can still see his face and the glint of the floodlights in the silver cup. The team celebrated with cups of tea in the dressing room – nearly all of them had to go to work early next day. I had to write my mock English literature A-Level, in Worcester, the next morning and it took ten minutes to clear the glittering glory images from my head so I could get down to writing about Shakespeare's imagery.

Back in 1981, Droitwich Spa FC didn't even exist. If the footballers of the town wanted to go to the final of the Worcestershire Senior Cup, they would have had to pay on the gate like everyone else.

The club formed as a mere Sunday morning team in 1985. In that year, Worcester City were still in their pomp, lording it at St George's Lane before thousands in the Alliance Premier League.

By contrast, Droitwich Spa took up Saturday afternoon football only in this century. To be fair, for most of its life, the club has been about as influential in football in Worcestershire as cricket is in New York.

Yet this fledgling club has risen rapidly through the ranks. Largely, thanks to sound infrastructure, shrewd investment, a touch of success and solid, growing, support.

The club has rebranded itself as the Salt Men.

Droitwich Spa, population 25,000, has been famous for its salt since Roman times.

When I was a child, I remember going with my family to the brine baths in Droitwich.

It was a night out we always looked forward to. You could float in the hot healing waters for a wonderful hour, the salt crusting on your chin.

The attendants wrapped you in hot towels after your dip, and you could sit for a few minutes. Warm and content in the wooden Victorian changing rooms along the side of the bath under a Gothic-style vaulted roof; simple pleasures.

Football clubs in Worcestershire used to use the brine baths for easing their players' tired muscles.

Droitwich brine has ten times more salt than seawater and is on a par with the Dead Sea. The name of the River Salwarpe, that flows through the town, is believed to be derived from the Latin: 'The river that throws up the salt.' Nearly 2,000 years after the Romans left, the football club is keen to use the small town's history – let's face it, it is famous for little else – to sell merchandise and help finance football.

So, this was the setting in Droitwich on 14 November 2023 for a revenge grudge match. The salty upstarts against the former aristocrats of the non-League game. It was never going to be an easy night in Droitwich Spa. Getting to the ground, a few miles from Worcester, was the first hurdle.

'It is a great ground to visit – if you can find it!' a veteran fan told me, with a laugh.

Sure enough, you wouldn't stumble across the ground. It is tucked away behind a leisure centre, not too far from the concrete-and-glass boxes of Droitwich High School.

Fair play, the club had laid on free parking at the school to help accommodate an unusually large number of cars.

To complicate matters, Droitwich Spa football ground can't be seen from the dark of the roadside. You have to seek directions and walk down a long, damp lane.

At the end of the lane, is a neat little ground, full of ambition and sponsorship. It is like many of the new wave of non-League grounds across the country: spartan, organised, with a high mesh fence looking a bit like a cross between a tennis court and an open prison.

These new grounds rarely see big crowds, which is just as well. They have no terracing, nor elevation, on three sides of the ground.

If you have a big crowd like the 949 who squeezed in on this night, people are left craning their necks to see over the heads bunched along the rail in the narrow space by the touchline.

If Droitwich is the future, it comes complete with numerous stewards and decent support in a ground the club scrimped and saved to buy.

At the very least, Droitwich Spa FC, unlike many at this level, can call the King George V ground its own with scope for expansion. It is a lesson for many other struggling nearby clubs including Worcester City and Stourbridge.

It took four years of humble exile by Droitwich for developers to turn an open sports field into the makings of a stadium.

Droitwich Spa played at nearby Stourport Swifts, while workers built a supporters' club, dressing rooms and a 100-seat stand. The club wanted two stands but could only afford one. The stand too far probably cost the same as a second-string defender in the lower reaches of the professional game.

'The few of us that have been here since the outset have had to take a deep breath – we can't believe that what we thought we could do has actually come off – it's amazing!' says Droitwich Spa vice-chairman Mark Bowen.

On this cold November night, Droitwich Spa supporters weren't holding their breath ahead of the visit of a Worcester City side; even though the visitors arrived on the back of a winning streak. The home fans behind the goal had a peculiar kind of unshakeable optimism.

'I've got it down for another 3-0 win!' said a Droitwich Spa supporter behind the goal as he pulled his woollen hat down against the cold. Other home supporters standing nearby seemed adamant their team was worth its salt.

Sure enough, 30 minutes into the game, Charlie Tilley took an outrageous shot from way out that seemed to be heading far into the starry night sky. Instead, it dipped and dropped into the back of the net to the surprise of everyone, especially the goalkeeper. 1-0.

'I thought it was going over the bar,' said the man in the woolly hat.

'I think he did too!' laughed an older fan standing next to him and pointing at the opposing goalkeeper. 'You never know in these games, do you?'

Just before half-time, Worcester City's lean, languid, two-footed terror of the wings Liam Lockett charged down the right and drilled the ball into the bottom corner of the net as if it was nothing.

'When he is bang at it he is unplayable, he will just run and run at the backs and they just cannot keep up with him, he is too quick, very direct as well,' says journalist Marcello Cossali-Francis, who reported on the Droitwich game that night.

'He gets the ball, turns and runs right at you and he is very hard to stop. And like you said, he is good with both feet, you never know what he is going to do. He can cut in and put it in top bins or just put it through your legs and run you ragged. He is relentless.'

Some of the City supporters feel Lockett telegraphs in that he raises his right hand when he is about to jink left with the ball. My view is Lockett, at this level, could play with both hands in his pockets and still stand a chance of skinning most defenders.

Lockett leapt before the City supporters as he levelled the score. When the applause had died down there was a brief pause.

'I'm revising my prediction to 3-1,' said he of the woolly hat. 'Maybe they will score two own goals!' We all laugh.

This man should not have worried, this was not going to be City's night whatever happened. Another 40 minutes of rearguard action by Worcester City came to an end in the 70th minute when youngster Roland Krol (I am showing my age, but I wonder if his team-mates call him Rudi?) leapt high to head the ball in from a corner.

'Could see it coming,' says the man next to me who, as a boy, had seen City play Sheffield United before 17,000 at St George's Lane in the FA Cup fourth round in 1959. I bet you, on that day, he didn't see a defeat to Droitwich Spa coming.

About ten minutes before the end, Nathan Binner stroked a penalty home, and the humiliation was complete as the night dew thickened on the pitch, dampening any optimism left among the travelling Worcester City supporters.

To be fair, on this night, Worcester City looked a bit jaded after more than a score of league and cup games. Certainly, they looked highly unlikely to lay any ghosts to rest against the lowly, noisy neighbours who proved considerably noisier as they left the pitch victorious.

At least the night finished with a few laughs. The ace in Droitwich Spa's hand was an offside trap that largely saw their defenders hold a line a couple of inches in from the halfway line.

It meant there were around 20 offside decisions against Worcester City. Probably half of them were questionable, to say the least.

It was so bad that frustrated City fans started shouting at the linesman and ended up laughing loudly every time the flag went up for another dodgy decision.

I have probably never heard, or seen, anything like it in more than half a century of watching non-League football. Extraordinary.

A number of City supporters gave the referee a piece of their mind as he left the pitch. Referees at this level earn around £60 a game for putting up with this kind of barracking and worse. Surely, it can't be worth the money.

You also have to hand it to the good-natured Droitwich supporters. There was no abuse or aggressive posturing during the game.

OK, it is easier to be magnanimous when you win. My abiding memory was smiling faces and good old-fashioned encouragement for a good crop of young players and a brave goalkeeper who looked like he was 12 but stopped shots like he was 30.

At the final whistle, Julian Pugh, the Worcester City historian, was sanguine about this forgettable little chapter in the club's history.

'You kind of accept you are where you are. Trying to think you are still big and special. So, in respect we have lost football matches in places I have never even heard of, never mind been to before. Quite clearly, the standard of football is as low as it has ever been, you have to sit there and accept the misery, you know. It is not going to stay like this forever, football goes up and down. I mean, if you are a Man United supporter the last two or three years haven't been that special.'

Droitwich Spa looked a lively and determined side of the future. They may be small fry in Worcestershire right now, but in five years' time they won't be and the club holds its destiny in its own hands in the shape of the modern ground that it owns.

This was probably not the last time Droitwich Spa would rub salt in Worcester City's wounds.

Chapter 11

Tough in Tuffley

A FEW weeks before, at the beginning of October, I followed scores of Worcester City fans down the M5 to Gloucestershire to see the return game at Tuffley Rovers.

At the start of the season, I had earmarked Glevum Park as a ground I had never been to and wanted to visit. Apart from that, the return game couldn't be worse than the 0-0 draw in Worcester in the first game of the season; besides, by this time Worcester City were second in the league and starting to look like contenders. Tuffley Rovers were second from bottom with only one win.

Tuffley, on the fringes of Gloucester, doesn't really fit the wealthy Gloucestershire image. The walk to the ground, tucked away in the middle of a housing estate, is through squat homes and prefabs with gnomes in the garden.

On the way to Glevum Park the ground, a late-middle-aged man stopped dead on the pathway on the opposite side of the street. He turned, looked straight at me and put his fingers up to his mouth. I looked back blankly; so, he did it again.

'Have you got a cigarette?' said he. It was probably the first time I'd been asked for a cigarette on the streets on England for about 40 years. I don't smoke.

On the news on the way down was Boris Johnson banging on about levelling up. You could argue Tuffley could do with a bit of that.

Glevum Park itself looks a bit basic, even as non-League grounds go, but homely. All around me, as I walk in are weathered faces who look like they could tell a thousand stories about supporting a non-League club down among the dead men.

The game kicked off. I stand behind the goal close enough to reach out and touch the players as they come up for a corner. That is non-League football, you get close enough to see the sweat and hear the panting.

One of the Tuffley Rovers players is pole-axed by the corner flag.

'Hey, do you want a cuddle?' says one of the knee-high kids behind the goal.

Worcester City's rising star Elliot Hartley and a couple of other players turn and laugh as they wait on the goal line for the ball. Imagine Bruno Fernandes doing that?

In the first 30 seconds visiting striker Kyle Belmonte misses a simple chance at the far post. Minutes later, City hit the crossbar; the pressure grows.

Ten minutes in, one in the eye for City; Tuffley midfielder Henry Birkett pulls an outrageous lob over the City keeper to make it 1-0, drawing a brusque cheer from the surprised home fans.

'We will win,' says a City fan standing next to me, unmoved.

'Come on Ell!' shouts one of the fans behind the goal and he does. The ball is worked down the left and crossed to the far post where Hartley drifts in to score the equaliser.

Just before half-time, disaster for the visitors; Tuffley Rovers break, Jake White rides a tackle about 30 yards out and holds his nerve in a one-on-one with the keeper to put the ball calmly into the bottom corner. 2-1.

In a frantic last few minutes of the first half Worcester City fight back and miss a couple of sitters and have one kicked off the line. Seconds before the whistle they drill in another shot. A fan shouts: 'That's it!' It isn't, the ball hits the post and bounces away.

Worcester City troop in at the break 2-1 down and wondering if winning this league is going to be that straightforward after all.

Not too long into the second half and Worcester City settle down before Hartley strikes again. Another long ball in from the left and Hartley glances a header into the bottom corner for his seventh goal in nine games.

Winger Liam Lockett sends City into the lead. A crisp passing move just outside the penalty area sets Lockett free and he guides the ball into the bottom corner off the right-hand post for his tenth goal in 17 games. It was one-way traffic from then as City hit the post yet again.

Another sweeping move across the park after a breakout from defence ended up at the feet of Belmonte, who buried it for his tenth in 11 games. A superb strike, to seal a superb comeback.

There were 224 supporters there on the night; I reckon more than half were from Worcester, who made the noise of 500 in a stadium with a mere 1,000 capacity.

It was nice at the end of the night. Many supporters from Worcester gathered as the players came off the field to cheer them off. You started to get the feeling that this may be a special season to remember after all.

Tuffley Rovers didn't have much to shout about at the end of the night, but at least the club owns its own ground ...

Chapter 12

How City Lost its Ground

I met my girl down St George's Lane
dreamed a dream, watched a game
I kissed my girl by the Canal End wall
They sold our own ground, sold our own ground

We'll follow our club wherever they go
but we need to go home
but the Council say NO
we'll fight the fight

won't be put down
we'll build our own ground, we'll build our own ground
we're coming home from this exiled hell
coming home to Perdiswell

to save our club we are duty bound
we'll build our own ground
build our own ground

Councillors come and Councillors go
it's us who put you there you know
so, when you're gone we'll still be round

to build our own ground build our own ground
build our own ground build our own ground
build our own ground build our own ground
build our own ground build our own ground

The outraged and pained lyrics of 'BringCityHome' by an outfit called CityPunk.

Wordsmiths are usually inspired to write songs about great wins and heroic players; rarely do songwriters write so passionately about their club being homeless.

This was the case when Worcester City lost their ground in 2013. They had to share a ground with deadly rivals Kidderminster Harriers; to add insult to injury, this was followed by a stint at fledgling rivals Bromsgrove Sporting.

It was tantamount to Napoleon being forced to drill his troops in a British barracks after the Battle of Waterloo and march them through the town on Saturdays.

One gloomy Saturday afternoon, current board member Dave Wood, an electrical design engineer who runs a company in the city, supped a post-match pint around the table with a bunch of other Worcester City supporters.

'It came from a crisis of depression. We sat round a table in the bar. FC United had done a version of "Dirty Old Town". We started singing it, stared putting words to it and basically a gang of us from the Supporters' Trust put the words together and wrote the song in an hour and a half,' he recalls.

'Getting on the train to go to Kidderminster Harriers to watch a home game and thinking, what's going on here?'

They took the song to a musician friend – Paz Smith, a former Worcester punk rocker from Warndon, now aged 62. He was one of the first people in Worcester to hear the Sex Pistols, in 1976, and made his debut with his punk band The Samples in the sweaty smoky cavern under the Golden Lion pub in the High Street in 1978. It always took time for punk to permeate the provinces.

Smith's band rose to support The Fall, including the late Mark E Smith, at Malvern Winter Gardens and more than 40 years later he hasn't lost his touch. He recorded the Worcester City song in his bedroom in nearby Droitwich, singing lead vocals and playing all the instruments himself. It was a simple GCD and E minor.

'It seemed to me it must have some bollocks and be guitar driven ... I probably recorded it in four hours.'

Richard Widdowson, of the Supporters' Trust, made the video – dragooning Wood in on guitar – and last time I looked it had about 6,500 views on YouTube, in just over a decade.

Not bad for a defiant lament for the deepest wound in Worcester City's 122-year history. The simple fact that it once owned one of the most imposing non-League grounds in the country and now it doesn't have so much as a cowfield to call its own. To make matters worse, the club yielded very little in return for selling off the family silver.

Growing debt forced the club's hand to commit that cardinal sin in football: selling off your ground before you get another one.

A combination of poor housekeeping, with a dash of bad luck, saw the proceeds trickle away in the decade leading to a tumble down several divisions, to near amateur football, on the way to the near-fatal penury of summer 2023.

Such a shame, as St George's Lane was as grand and celebrated as the saint himself.

In its heyday, you could see the lights for miles. It seemed the ground was worth every penny the club paid for it.

Worcester City bought St George's Lane from a family living next door to the ground for £3,000 in 1947. It took a £300 deposit and then the club was able to start developing the ground, building terraces and capacity.

Yet, by the end of the 20th century St George's Lane was looking a bit worse for wear. The safety and ground requirements to stay in the top stream of non-League football were getting more expensive ever year.

'It was old and falling down, and needed a lot of money for repairs,' says David Boddy, a former club chairman.

The job was a dream come true for Boddy, the blood in his veins was blue and white. He was always a football man first and foremost and a Worcester City man through and through. He saw his first game at St George's Lane the age of nine against Wimbledon.

When we were young nobodies on the terraces at St George's Lane, he always put his arms forward and shouted: 'Come on you blues!' as the players ran out. I remember in 1979, when City lost in the last minute away to Salisbury in the FA Cup, Boddy wore a black armband to Worcester Technical College on Monday morning. There can be few who took Worcester City so much to heart.

All Boddy wanted in life was to work in football.

'What are you doing with a tinpot football club, eh?' our economics lecturer used to say.

Boddy started out as a commercial manager with Bromsgrove Rovers, followed by Worcestershire County Cricket Club, City, Newport County and a stint as chief executive at Coventry City from 2017 to 2024 overseeing a rise from League Two to the Championship.

Boddy was chairman at Worcester City in 2003 as the board was talking to property companies and working out valuations.

Down the years he has been castigated by the fans accusing him of handling the ground issue poorly and alleging he took money out of the club. Boddy has strenuously denied both.

'Well what people first of all have to remember, is that it was all completely voluntary, I never got paid a penny for any of it,' he says one afternoon in the Swan in Whittington, a village just outside Worcester.

'On average we had 10 directors, at one point we had 12, they contribute X amount to things we have to do. We had to pay for things ... on average, in an average year, putting all those things together it came to about £6,000 to £7,000 each, but there were other things I had to do on top of that, or didn't have to do, put money and support into things, but I wasn't the only one, we were all working-class people with not much money to throw around.

'Mike Sorensen put an awful lot of money in over a load of time, he was chairman before me, and he remained as a director. When something needs buying and you can't afford to buy it, someone needs to put their hand in their pocket and buy it.'

Boddy says he chipped in to buy midfielder Adam Wilde from Cambridge United.

'The major, major factor was we were over £650,000 in debt when I joined the board. During my tenure at the club that rose to a million, so we can't walk away from that. You have got to own that fact and take responsibility for what happened but you're battling against the tide,' says Boddy.

'When you've got an overdraft like that, it is a noose around your neck. At one point we were paying £1,000 a week interest on that money. So, £52,000 in interest, before you kick a football. It hurts, but the most important fact of today and for the whole story really, is we banked with NatWest Royal Bank of Scotland, and they wanted the money back, simple as that.'

The value of St George's Lane had to be realised, and talks went ahead as early as 2001. The ground was prime housing land, in a quiet corner of the city, close to the centre.

The Supporters' Trust claims the ground was valued at as much as £8.2m in 2007.

For a club which had survived two world wars and numerous recessions, the ground sale was going to be a painful, debilitating battle.

It all should have been so simple. In 2008, Careys New Homes, a family business based in Wembley, agreed a deal for £7.36m for St George's Lane, enough then to build a fine stadium in the city.

Property company St Modwen was working on a new home for Worcester City on the outskirts of the city at a site in Nunnery Way near the M5.

Widdowson says the supporters opposed the deal to the bitter end: 'We did our best to stop it … We did our homework; we knew it inside out. We knew everything that was going on, we knew what was in the contracts. We tried to stop the contracts being signed. We tried to get people to look at what they were proposing and that none of it made sense.'

'We said, "Dave, this ain't right; people will admire you for stepping backwards and saying this ain't right." He wouldn't, he wanted to be the man who took Worcester City to a new football ground.'

On the face of it, Nunnery Way was ideal; out of town with open roads around it. The idea was a 6,000-capacity stadium with an advert painted on the roof to be seen by passing traffic on the M5 banked up above the ground.

There were plans to play Liverpool in the first game.

It seemed like a dream solution. It depended upon Careys New Homes getting permission for 98 new homes on St George's Lane.

Sadly, it wasn't that simple.

Seasoned Worcester-based lawyer David Hallmark, working pro bono, was brought in to work on the Nunnery Way stadium bid with the pressure from the banks growing for a sale of St George's Lane to repay the debt. By 2009, that debt had ballooned to £1.5 million.

'I believe the board thought we have got all this money coming, so we can spend and it is OK,' says lifelong supporter and guitarist Wood.

Top priority for the club was a new home, according to Hallmark, who reckoned the club wouldn't be left with enough money to pay off debts and build a new stadium. 'And we recognised that we couldn't and therefore it needed to be a joint venture with other people building on the site, which share the infrastructure, the roads, the drainage, the sewers, the electricity, all the facilities,' says Hallmark 15 years later.

DIY superstore B&Q liked the idea. Their nearest store was in Halesowen, and they wanted to get into Worcester, in a site with good traffic access. New B&Q stores tend to bring traffic with them. Hallmark held meetings with B&Q and the head of planning at Worcester City Council.

'He [the head of planning] said: "I don't want a B&Q there." And then we said: "Well, why not?" He couldn't actually say why not except that it wasn't in the local plan to have a B&Q on the edge of that side of Worcester. So can you change your local plan? No, we can't. So, we then got into the situation where we spoke with B&Q and went and met the B&Q people somewhere down south and they said, "No, we're keen. This is a site we're prepared to risk, we're prepared to support it," says Hallmark.

To complicate matters Worcestershire Highways insisted that a footbridge must be constructed over the highway to the football ground at a cost of a million pounds to the club. On the ground, opposition was growing.

'The nightmare for people who are not soccer followers and we've all seen it on the television; the football crowds park where they want to park, park in front of your house, park on your car parking space,' says Hallmark, who eventually took the planning application to appeal.

'Essentially an estate nearby famously decided they would object to a football stadium on the grounds that it was nearby to their park, and I argued on behalf of the football club. It wasn't nearby to their park, there was a motorway between them. And the only impact on noise would be suffered by the deer and the daffodils!' he says.

Both the application and appeal were thrown out.

'There were going to be shops and stores and little businesses underneath the stand. It was a circular stadium. It would have been a high-profile, pretty building, which would have done good for the city and the club. But nobody wanted us,' concludes Hallmark.

Boddy resigned as chairman in 2009, saying he could take the club no further. He denied it was anything to do with a fan petition calling for his resignation. For years afterwards he was subjected to small town abuse from fans.

'I vividly remember, coming out the County Ground one day, and I'm walking down New Road, with 1,000 other people on the Cripplegate Park side the road, and on the other side of the road is this faceless wanker who shouts something like: "Boddy, fucking tosser!" or something like that across the road. This is five years after I have left City and I've got regrets about that,' he says.

'I was in a pub one Sunday night, in the Anchor, in Diglis in Worcester, with my kids in the garden, and one twat wanted to start shouting at me from the corner, and I don't need, want or deserve that, and they still want to do it; and they still think its OK to do it, but they are faceless wankers.'

Hallmark also left after the planning disappointment, but not before he had persuaded a new chairman to join.

'David Hallmark said can you come on to the board as chairman and get this thing out of the shit,' says Anthony Hampson, who took over from Boddy as chairman and oversaw the final countdown to the controversial ground sale.

'I didn't know anything about the niceties of football, or running a club, or anything. I was just a sort of a businessman,' says Hampson on a crisp November morning at his office in the shadow of the Malvern Hills.

My elders would have called Hampson 'Old Worcestershire money'. Yet he started his working life at the old livestock market in the Butts, in the centre of Worcester, which is now a car park.

'I used to mark the cattle with different coloured paint for an auctioneer,' he says with a smile.

There was also a family business, Diglis Trading Estate by the river in the south of the city, which he ran. Three factories, including manufacturing and engineering, one of which is still standing.

Why did Hallmark ask someone to step in who cared little for football, I ask?

'He knew I could do it as a businessperson; he didn't have a clue. None of his people had a clue; David Boddy didn't have a clue,' says Hampson.

'What Dave Boddy did to Worcester City, Liz Truss did to the nation,' he says with a laugh.

'They were going around like headless chickens, no focus on getting the money in.

'The bar, the money was not controlled by the club and someone was taking the proceeds from the bar. The sports shop was non-existent. We managed to straighten the shop out. The only thing I saw was money going out of the club,' says Hampson.

I put this to his predecessor Boddy.

'Anthony Hampson's comments about my business acumen are disappointing and disrespectful. My record prior to joining the Worcester City Board of Building, then selling my successful Sportslines business to ClubCall, then being responsible for multi-million-pound budgets at ClubCall is proven. Then after leaving the City, my success at both Newport County AFC and Coventry City FC is there for all to see,' he says.

'His suggestion that the board, of which I was chairman, was spending money like water is simply not true; we were as prudent as possible, whilst trying to remain competitive, against a legacy debt that was snowballing.'

For the next ten years it would be Hampson's difficult job not only to shore up Worcester City's finances, but oversee the handover of St George's Lane to the bulldozers and housing developers. It was to make him as unpopular with the supporters as his predecessor.

Chapter 13

There'll Be 50,000 People Parking on our Lawn

'HAMPSON OUT! Hampson Out!'

It was Saturday afternoon at a crowded platform at Worcester Foregate Street station in the heart of the city. The chant was from a bunch of Worcester City supporters returning from yet another game in unpopular exile at Bromsgrove Sporting.

'Hampson Out! Hampson Out!' they chanted at the urbane Worcester City chairman Anthony Hampson at the other end of the platform.

'It was appalling ... After a bit, I used to clap along with it,' says the man himself more than 15 years later.

'Talk about abuse, these days you would get a video of it and get plod to deal with it.

'We had a bit of a respite when we got the cup runs that shut everyone up for about three years. By 2013, it was getting unpleasant with the prospect of playing at Kidderminster. Meanwhile, money was haemorrhaging out of the club.'

Hampson's job was to staunch the flow of money out of the club as well as finalise the details of the sale of the ground. In its last years at St George's Lane, he says the club was haemorrhaging cash to the tune of up to £8,000 a month.

'You may as well have poured it down a plug,' he says.

'But we had no cash, it was just hand-to-mouth, so the fourth match in and suddenly I was running this club and I could see it going tits up, so I went into the changing room after the game, I can't remember which game it was. I remember vividly the floor was slightly scruffy; my glasses were steamed up because it was an old-fashioned dressing room, steam everywhere, men's bodies everywhere. I said, "Alright boys, I need to speak to you about the pay. The club is in the shit, we have had to pay your wages in cash. You will have to go to the cashier, after the game and by the way I am going to have to halve your money by next week." "Whaaaaat?', said the players.'

Hampson questioned all of the increasing costs of football in the National League.

'A lot of clubs at that level were saying, "Guys, we can't afford two grand for a coach to Bradford Park Avenue." You were playing Workington and it was a coach for two days, a hotel bill – another thousand pounds. Money literally drains out of the club very rapidly when it is trying to box above its weight and that was the problem with Worcester City.'

In the early days Hampson also motored north to Edinburgh to see the club's biggest creditor, the Royal Bank of Scotland.

'I drove up to their offices and they wanted to pull the plug on the whole thing. It was only that I had got involved and they knew my background that they held off and allowed the deal to go through and that's what happened. They kept continuing to lend the club money, on and on and on, because they knew they had the security of the ground.

'They could have taken the whole shooting match.'

This is one reason why Hampson refutes the claim of some Worcester City fans that the club didn't have to sell St George's Lane.

'There is no point maintaining that. It would have been a slow death, a gradual draining to the fact that the original directors before me kept going to RBS and they kept shunting more money in. We got no choice but to sell it.'

The housing deal brought a little cash into the club. Careys New Homes paid £65,000 a year to the club for the first three years.

'That basically was a down payment, robbing Peter to pay Paul. It kept us afloat, kept us going,' says Hampson.

Following the collapse of the Nunnery Way planning application, the Supporters' Trust was putting together a new application for a site in Perdiswell in the north of the city.

Richard Widdowson, of the Supporters' Trust, was one of the leaders of the Perdiswell plan and oversaw the drawing up of pictures and went-door to door to support it.

The planning application was heard by Worcester City Council in 2017. Three studies said the ground was suitable and the club spent £57,000 on preparing the application.

'We went to council, went down to a chairman's casting vote and it got thrown out.

'We went to appeal, won the appeal, but the council didn't want it,' says Widdowson.

'The rug was pulled from under us. People living on the estate near where we were going to build objected saying we were going to build Old Trafford in Perdiswell. There will be 50,000 people parking on our garden and pissing on our lawn and shooting our cats, or whatever.'

Hampson poured more cold water on the Perdiswell plan and the Supporters' Trust.

'They were a complete disaster. All they wanted to do was criticise, pull the thing to pieces and give me absolutely no support at all. I am a people person and I wanted to get to know them all and be pally with them and everything else, but they wanted to push this Perdiswell project. That cost us £65,000 because they wouldn't stop. I said: "You are not going to get it, the council is not going to give you that bit of land. You are wasting your time."

'They had drawings done with pictures of trees and people walking past with dogs. Architects, surveyors and meetings,' says Hampson.

'It was pie in the sky – never going to happen!'

Then came Parsonage Way, a proposal by the club for a ground on a wet piece of land near the old church in Warndon.

'The ground is basically a marsh,' says Widdowson. It never went anywhere either.

The club also looked into the prospect of sharing Sixways, the home of the then top-flight rugby side Worcester Warriors. A delegation went to the House of Lords to meet the Football Association to discuss ground sharing, only to be told that under English law football enjoyed so-called 'primacy' over rugby. This means that if Worcester City was playing Walsall Wood on the same day as Worcester Warriors played Saracens, the rugby club would have to cancel its fixture. Not surprisingly, the rugby club got cold feet. In December 2024 Worcester City did sign a ground sharing deal with the owners of Sixways.

When the sale of St George's Lane came through it was as disappointing as it was controversial. The £7.46m price tag had fallen to around £3.2m because of the failure to gain planning permission for 98 houses on the football ground site. On top of this there had been a plunge in the land values in the wake of the 2008 financial crisis.

Two million pounds of that money went to pay off the bank debt and the rest had to be prised away from the proposed developer at Nunnery Way – St Modwen.

'The football club never got the money, it went straight to the developer and he developer was sitting on the money when the transaction went through,' recalls Hampson.

'So, they had all the power. So, I had to get out of the contract with St Modwen because they were sitting on our money, and they charged us something like £500,000 to get out of the contract. So when we finalised the whole thing and paid St Modwen their £500,000, we had only £600,000, so all we got for the whole shenanigans was £600,000. That was it.

'What would have appeared a decent wedge was reduced down to just £600,000 with no certainty of going somewhere else.'

There was even less in the bank by the time the final game at St George's Lane came against Chester City on 27 April 2013.

Grown men wept in the stands that day. The end of 108 years of football on the hallowed turf of a ground which hosted big names including Sir Stanley Matthews and the heavyweight boxing champion Tommy Farr. The Tonypandy Terror beat Austrian heavyweight Jo Wieden on points before a huge crowd in 1952, despite being knocked down in the seventh round.

GIs played American football on St George's Lane; there was motorcycle football, wrestling and floodlit cricket.

In all, people paid nearly five million times to watch football at St George's Lane. From that day in April no more. An uncertain future, pretty much penniless and certainly homeless. The bulldozers moved in the following month.

Not many people know this, as Michael Caine would say, but during Hampson's time Worcester City had a fleeting chance to buy a football ground outright in cash.

That is the good news, the bad news it was an offer for Claines Lane, the bog upon which the club currently plays.

Hampson says he went to the council to say he was prepared to buy Claines Lane for £120,000, the price of a terraced house in Worcester, and had a meeting with a number of people at County Hall.

'They said it's not enough; we want double that. I said I'm sorry but I have done my very best. They were orginally asking £120,000; could have done that out of the St George's Lane money. The Worcestershire FA ended up buying it.

'It is a really good facility. The problem is the club don't own it,' he says.

'There they are [the fans] because they were draining on this Perdiswell project, draining any spare dosh and I was losing the will to live. I didn't have the energy just to say stop, otherwise they would have had effigies of me round by the Cathedral with pins on my head,' he says with a laugh.

Hampson's time with the club ended in 2018 with the team still playing in exile and the bank balance low.

'They came up to me and said, 'Anthony, we want you to resign.' I said, "Alright then, where's the bit of paper?"'

Chapter 14

The Pain of Playing on a Paddy Field

IN MANY ways, the club can count its lucky stars that former chairman Anthony Hampson didn't buy Claines Lane. Even a tenancy there is a nightmare.

'Twas a few days before Christmas and it as was cold as charity, as my late and wise grandmother used to say.

For the whole day, a storm lashed the city of Worcester.

Out on the night streets of the city, little made a sound, nothing stirred, not even a mouse, not even an outraged keyboard warrior.

Most people were cosy behind closed doors, with the heating turned up. Along the Droitwich Road out of Worcester, on the way to Claines Lane the flashing Christmas lights blinked like swarms of fireflies in the gardens of every other suburban home. Pools of warm light beamed through the windows as families settled back ready for Christmas Eve.

Worcester City also had an inner glow this Christmas. It was December 2023, less than six months after the club almost died in penury, the team was top of the league, albeit on goal difference, with a handful of games in hand.

Yet, on this stormy night, many fans were equally blustery. Their biggest gripe lay under the feet of their talented, table-topping team. For weeks, supporters spat annoyance on social media at Worcester City's landlords at Claines Lane over the state of the pitch.

The 130-year-old Worcestershire Football Association (WFA) guides the destiny of 1,100 football clubs and more than 20,000 players in the county, as well as heaven knows how many thousands of volunteers that keep the game going.

The WFA also ploughed nearly £3m into making Claines Lane into a passable non-League ground, but couldn't stop the flooding.

The online comedians had been out in force for weeks with underwater pictures of frogmen with the caption: 'A pitch inspection at Claines Lane.' Ho, ho.

Top of the league, or not, it was going wrong, they said online: the soggy pitch; the stands, or lack of them; and a tannoy that you can't hear on matchdays. The latter complaint could probably be levelled against every non-League club in the country. I always say, they could announce your own mother's birthday at half-time, and you would be none the wiser.

The WFA – a bit like a branch of the civil service – decided it was time to consult with its stakeholders, after weeks of online criticism. In English, talk to the people who ultimately put down their money to pay for the game: the long-suffering supporters.

On arrival, there were mince pies and hot coffee in the modern concrete and glass WFA buildings at Claines Lane overlooking the pitch. A good bit of PR to set the tone.

Twinkling Christmas stars hung from the bar as WFA chief operating officer Ollie Williams, a former goalkeeping coach for Kidderminster Harriers, and his boss Nichola Trigg the chief executive, stood before a dozen supporters – ready for anything.

Trigg, a qualified chartered accountant with a robust character, has been with the WFA for more than 11 years. She is a qualified referee, trained to deal with dissent; just as well.

'We are here in peace,' says Williams to set the tone of the meeting.

They were also in luck. I expected a posse of angry keyboard warriors ready to stand up, raise voices and jab fingers.

Instead, there came forth a group of fairly elderly men, bearing mild criticism; more welcome to the WFA, after months of abuse, than the three kings bearing gold, frankincense and myrrh.

First and last was the state of the pitch. The officials told the meeting that the pitch went for 40 years without a proper roll, or cut, before City moved in.

The problem is the pitch holds more water than a reservoir. Some fans have nicknamed it the paddy field.

The new owner of the club Simon Lancaster cut his teeth at Claines Lane as a creative central midfielder for Worcester City juniors.

'I grew up playing on that pitch, as a kid, before it was a stadium, like it is now, and it's always been a bog, you know, because it's on a hill and the rain runs down it and there's a bloody big pond in the corner. I mean, so it is, it's always going to be a bog, and it is what it is. Do I think we could probably improve the situation by putting drainage in? Yes, but it won't guarantee every game. With the rain we have had the last couple of weeks, (it had been pouring that December and the river was in flood) you could put in all the drainage in the world and you won't be playing on it this past couple of weeks,' he told me just after the meeting.

This water has put paid to many games, in this rainy 2023/24 season, costing the club a pile of gate money. One cup game was washed out twice at Claines Lane; the authorities switched it to the away team, meaning a loss of revenue to Worcester City.

The problem is there is clay under the pitch that holds the water in. It means even a heavy shower can leave you paddling down the pitch hours before a game.

The WFA has chipped in, with the club, to pour £25,000 worth of sand on the pitch to try to soak up the water. At times, the pitch looked like a beach, says Trigg.

'Why don't we rip it all up?' says a voice from the floor.

'Even if we do it out of season, it will be October before you can play a game on it,' replies Trigg.

'What about a cover when it rains?,' says another grey-bearded supporter.

'We have tried, but it didn't work. We can't afford to invest in a new cover,' says Trigg.

'Why don't we ask the cricket club if we can borrow one of theirs?'

'Maybe,' says Williams slowly as he makes a note to write to Worcestershire County Cricket Club at New Road, on the other side of the city. We hold our breath.

Months later, at the end of March, Worcester City did ask the cricket club for a cover ahead of the FA Vase semi-final home first leg against Great Wakering Rovers from Essex. The problem was the cover only covered a quarter of the ground.

Result? Match postponed.

Then there was the stands. How many people, me included, are rained upon behind the goal at the far end of the ground?

That end is as open as in the days when I used to drive up on Sunday morning to watch my college mates play for County Sports, more than 40 years ago.

To cap it off, there is no elevation for supporters on three sides of the ground, leaving supporters craning over the crowded heads of others when the ground has more than a few hundred in it.

Trigg replies it would have cost £35,000 to put a stand behind the goal. One of the economies that had to be made when eking out the £3m set aside to build the ground.

'The cost of that stand is now more than £50,000. All these things are eye-wateringly expensive,' she says.

'We are well aware of the limitations of the ground, but we simply can't do everything at once.'

Journalists weren't invited to this little gathering. I was there as a paying customer of Worcester City.

One of the journalists who missed out that night was Marcello Cossali-Francis, then of the *Worcester News*. He had been writing about Worcester City and the struggles of the WFA for years and I clued him in about what happened at the meeting.

'That seems to have been their approach the whole time: "We are doing what we can." But nobody is seeing that in action.

'I have been to other FA pitches that have been so much better. You have got other places around Worcester that do not have as much money as them and the pitch is so much better. Why is that the case?' he says.

Then, finally, the tannoy. No one in the ground can understand a word that comes out of it, including me.

Trigg says it is fine when there are small crowds, but admits the tannoy crackles into oblivion when there is a big crowd. Her theory is that when there is a large number of mobile phones being used signals interfere with the crackling announcements that no one seems to be able to hear.

'We think this is what it is, but we don't know for sure,' she says.

Please could they make an announcement when they find out, or better still, put it up on the notice board where we can read it.

WFA over and out.

Five days later in that cold December, the water curse returned to haunt Worcester City. Rain storms swept the city in the run up to Christmas.

On Boxing Day, City were to play city rivals Worcester Raiders, a new club from the other side of the tracks, at Claines Lane.

The omens ahead of this game had been so favourable. Three days before, Worcester City had played their main championship rivals: Corsham Town, from Wiltshire, before a healthy crowd of 780. Just a year before, you would have to pay people to get that many through the turnstiles for a Worcester City match.

Corsham missed a penalty early in the first half. At the other end, City's Dylan Hart glanced a header to give the home side a first-half lead.

Corsham came back eight minutes into the second half. The visitors took advantage of chaos in the penalty box to equalise with a drilled shot from 15 yards out.

Then, in the 69th minute, Worcester City got the goal their supporters longed for, and their players had threatened to score for most of the second half.

As often happens at this level, a long ball forward. Fleet-footed veteran striker Izak Reid, who ten years before was playing professional football for Morecambe in League Two, latched onto a through ball and smashed it low past the Corsham keeper. 2-1.

Corsham came within a split ace of an equaliser but couldn't stop Worcester City going back to the top of the table at Christmas, with games in hand.

A sweet appetiser for Boxing Day, many thought. Claines Lane was all set for what promised to be one of the games of the season, against Worcester Raiders.

More than a thousand tickets sold out, a week before.

Then, the rain with a vengeance.

From 7.30 in the morning, on matchday, a team of volunteers were out on the pitch, in Wellingtons, trying to sweep gallons upon gallons of water from the grass. To no avail. Despite all of their valiant efforts, the ball stuck to the soggy pitch like glue.

The referee called the game off in the morning.

'I was disappointed with the Boxing Day game I think most pitches would have got that game on really, that was a frustrating one, but I mean the two weeks since, with the deluge we have had there is no pitch with all the drainage in the world that would get those games on,' says Lancaster, who has been looking at new drainage systems to go under the pitch at Claines Lane.

'Essentially you go down and the pipes are underneath and they take it off, it's sort of like a drainage system. We've had some quotes and they're coming out at about £30–40,000. But it's one of them, do we want to spend that on it if we might only be there for another year, you know? Do the WFA want to spend on it? Probably not, you know. Are there grants we can get for it, maybe, so it might be a combination of all three.'

Despite the stakeholder consultation and coffee at Claines Lane a few days before, the keyboard warriors – on Facebook – were on manoeuvres again in the wake of the Boxing Day Worcester Raiders washout. The season of goodwill was wearing thin.

'WFA not fit for purpose,' said one.

'Might as well call off the next two home matches now,' quipped another.

'Looks like they are keeping cows on that pitch. Typical WFA involvement, amateur at best.'

'What an embarrassing situation for the WFA, disgusting.'

The well-meaning officials must have wondered where all the warm feeling of their night of coffee, candour and mince pies went to.

Many supporters made their way to Claines Lane in the cold on Boxing Day, anyway, to buy a few pints and some of the food which cooks had prepared for the sell-out crowd.

The club gave the leftovers to the Maggs Day Centre, which helps the homeless of the city.

A warm gesture, on a cold December day, that surely speaks volumes about football in the community.

In the run up to the New Year, Worcester City finally ran for cover as the storms and rain sent the River Severn into raging flood. It left large parts of the city, especially the racecourse and cricket ground, looking like a small sea.

The day after the frustration of the Worcester Raiders game, 27 December, the club issued a statement saying it was going to stage the next two home games a few miles from home, on Malvern Town's plastic pitch.

Most supporters on Facebook were in favour.

'Well done, sense at last,' said one.

You can only speculate how much more difficult it would be to sell the idea of spending money travelling to another town to watch home games, if Worcester City had been on a losing streak. Imagine.

Luckily, Worcester City won one and drew the other in Malvern to cement their place at the top of the league for entertaining football to compensate for being at the bottom of the league of dry pitches.

Chapter 15

Beggars Can't Be choosers

THE PLAN to get away from the Claines Lane bog needs the patience of Job.

This was step one. The concerned crowd, full of frowns and foreboding, filed through the doors of Fernhill Heath Memorial Hall.

Outside, rain washed the pavements of the small village on the fringes of Worcester; ironically, at the same time creating another paddy field pudding back at Claines Lane. One of the main reasons why Worcester City set out its stadium stall before the villagers of Fernhill Heath.

On this cold wet night, 22 February 2024, all were here to look at the prospect of turning an open muddy field, just down the road, into the next – maybe permanent – stadium for Worcester City Football Club.

A dream new football ground with a capacity up to 4,000 with houses, car parks and maybe a new ground for Worcestershire County Cricket Club. A new home needed by the fans like a downpour in a drought, after more than a decade of ground shifting and sharing: from Kidderminster Harriers to Bromsgrove Rovers; it was embarrassing.

This uncomfortable tenure, squatting in the homes of rivals, came to an end only when the club moved back to Worcester to the soggy, unsuitable pitch at Claines Lane, in 2020.

The future lay in Fernhill Heath, thought the club. The muddy field in question was a car boot sale site down a narrow country track called Hurst Lane.

The biggest problem? It is smack bang in the middle of the green belt, the name of the protected swathes of green fields, ring fenced by the authorities across the country for decades, which stop towns and cities merging into one ugly huge urban sprawl.

In recent years, critics of the green belt say it restricts the supply of land for building, leading to a housing shortage and a steep rise in the cost of buying a home.

One of the passionate supporters of a new home for Worcester City is club sponsor and Worcester toyshop owner Tim Evans.

'We just need to be masters of our own destiny. For me, almost the first thing I said when Lancaster showed up was: "He is putting in his money, which is great for players, but what about the ground?" My first question was, has he got a plan for the ground?' says Evans.

'Getting our own ground is more important than promotion, because without it we won't go anywhere ... Ideally, you want your club as central as possible so everyone can walk there, but the cost of central property means it is never going to happen. So, you have to go on a motorway on the outskirts of town.'

Most fans agree.

'Hope it goes through, this is our only hope,' says one fan as he catches my eye at the door of Fernhill Heath Memorial Hall.

Some hope. Most of the Fernhill Heath residents came not to praise plans for a new stadium, but to bury them.

On the walls on one side of the room were pictures from City's glorious past. The teeming and jubilant 15,000 crowd at the triumph over Liverpool in 1959; the great players of the 1970s when Worcester City was one of the most feared non-League sides in the land; Paul Moss, the clever and nimble striker who scored for fun in the 1980s; fans celebrating an FA Cup equaliser against Scunthorpe earlier in this century.

Yet most of those milling around the hall couldn't have cared less or noticed if Paul Moss had walked into the room and stood in front of his picture.

'How many cars are we talking on matchday?' says one tetchily. 'Those are country lanes that can't handle that kind of traffic.'

'You will get rubbish thrown around and people will just park anywhere.'

People didn't say it in the hall on this night, but privately they fear drunken fans stalking the streets of Fernhill Heath on matchdays: throwing cans and decency to the wind.

Thousands more maybe from Lincoln City, Wrexham and Walsall if Worcester City – as planned – progress up the leagues.

'I'm a property developer and I do these kind of projects all over the country,' says one female resident with a smile.

'Could it work?' says I.

'Yes, but not in my backyard!'

Many of the residents who look over the plans on the tables seem to take issue – period – with the idea of a football ground on their doorstep.

'At least people are taking the trouble to lay out their plans and give you a chance to have your say,' I venture.

'We still don't like them,' says another elderly Fernhill Heath resident, without a smile.

'There is a lot of resistance to it. It is a small place and the idea of building something as big as they are proposing is a bit of a dream at this stage,' says journalist Marcello Cossali-Francis.

'This idea of Fernhill Heath as a concept looks great, you have got this massive Worcestershire sports park with cricket pitches and football pitches, indoor leisure centre and retirement living. Basically, we are talking about building a new town with Worcester City at the centre. In theory it all sounds great, but a lot of city fans know there is a long way to go.'

'I think it could take five years, even if it finds favour with the council,' says a long-standing City fan weeks after the Fernhill Heath Memorial Hall gathering.

The man bankrolling the proposed new home for City feels the people can be won over. People say of him he is a bit like Marmite; you either like him, or you don't.

Well, I like Marmite, have done so since I was a kid, and spent a good half hour chatting and laughing with him in Fernhill Heath; he is a remarkable character.

Stennard Harrison is a tall, larger-than-life, multi-millionaire developer, who is Worcester born-and-bred. He says, with a laugh, there were only three Stennard Harrisons in the world: himself, his father and grandfather.

His father, known to many of us growing up in Worcestershire as Scrappy Harrison, built a famous family-owned scrapyard in Lowesmoor, on the eastern edge of the city. Harrison says his father, now in his 80s, is retired and living in Spain.

'We did very well until Margaret Thatcher killed the British steel industry,' he says.

The family business is where Harrison started, as a 15-year-old fresh from school, pushing a broom in the scrapyard.

We laugh at the idea that working for your father is an easy life.

'I used to tell my dad that all my mates were going out on the town and he used to reply: "Yard!" and that was it!'

As the scrap business waned, Harrison went into the property development game, with gusto, with his company Marsten Developments.

Unlike many property developers, he says he only does projects in the city of his birth. As we spoke, Harrison had just completed a flat complex in Silver Street. In all, he says, he had £300m worth of building projects on the go in Worcester.

The proposed new stadium for Worcester City is among his most recent and ambitious; also, it is the most likely to go down in history. The press release calls it a visionary plan.

'Our master plan prioritises sustainability, incorporating green infrastructure and connection with pedestrian, cycle and public transport routes. It proposes a mix of sports pitches, green amenity, eco homes and extra care facilities,' said Harrison in the press release.

Marsten Developments brought in big-hitting town planners CarneySweeney in an attempt to transform the plan into bricks and mortar.

By April 2024, the experts were still finalising a plan to submit to the planning committee at Wychavon District Council. It is expected to be put before the planning committee before the end of 2024, but at Christmas it had still not happened.

The idea is to build up to a 565-seater Worcester Community Sports Park, with terracing for 660 fans. This would mean the stadium would be able to host matches right up to the non-League step one: the National League.

The club also believes, from day one, the stadium will be able to handle the average attendance over the last 40 years of 900 spectators.

The new stadium complex could also host Worcestershire County Cricket Club matches. The cricket club looked for a new home, in 2024, as it started yet another season with the famous New Road pitch under several feet of water, as the River Severn burst its banks after a wet spring. A groundsman once netted a salmon as it swam across the flooded ground.

Yet the cricket experts in the city say it is not practical and will take at least three years to bed down a wicket fit for first-class cricket.

The crux of the plan is to leverage the planning permission for the stadium with an application for up to 250 new homes on the green belt land.

The secret sauce in the deal is that Harrison – who is proud of his Worcester roots – is prepared to gift the stadium to the club, a magnanimous gesture from a hard-headed businessman which could turn out to be one of those rare footprints people leave in life.

This could also overcome Worcester City's greatest problem. It doesn't have any money to buy the land, let alone build a stadium; a bill that could run into millions.

Not surprisingly Simon Lancaster, the owner of Worcester City, who grew up in Fernhill Heath, is cautious about the plan; as any insurance man would be.

Lancaster says, if successful, he will take care to sign the lease of the ground over to the Supporters' Trust to ensure that the fans keep hold of their ground come what may.

'Well, I think it looks OK. Obviously, it's not where you'd pick it if you had your pick of the whole of Worcester. You'd probably go back to St George's Lane, but that's not available, nor anywhere close. The pickings are slim, so beggars can't be choosers, but where we're at, I think it looks OK. I was up with Sten, just before Christmas, you know, it's on a main road, there's a bus stop in Fernhill Heath, there's lots of parking; we've got parking in the plans,' he says, addressing one of the major objections of residents.

It was all so easy for Worcester City when the club moved into St George's Lane back in 1905. There was no stringent planning requirements, nor cars, nor ground regulations. People walked to the ground, or rode bikes from their homes in the nearby streets of Worcester. It wasn't a problem.

The club simply secured the lease of a meadow from a family who lived in the street next door and built a few stands and steps around the pitch. It was an easier, simpler time.

In the 21st century meadows are few and far between in Worcester and they are very expensive; there always seem to be groups of residents ready to fight football grounds.

'I think any development of this size is going to get some opposition. The whole country agrees we need more housing, on any political show that you watch – "we need more housing, we need more housing" – the politicians have said: "Yeah we've got to authorise more housing on green belt etc etc." Everyone agrees on that, but the trouble is no one wants it on their doorstep, they want it on the green belt down the road, don't they?' says Lancaster.

'We all want it, but we don't want it outside our house and that's just the way it is, you know. And I think that will be the same with this. If you're going to ask someone do they want a football stadium and 200 houses outside their house they'll probably say no!

Looking on the bright side, if the planners say yes, it could open the way for Worcester City to fashion their own ground with piles of cash from the moneybags professional game. Money could flow to Worcester from the wealthy Football Foundation. This is the money of the Premier League and the Football Assocation, which deliver grants for grassroots facilities and better places to play.

Heaven knows, this country's sprawling cities need better places to kick a ball in backed by development teams, if England is to have any chance of staying anywhere near the top of the world game in this century.

Since its creation in 2000, the Football Foundation has awarded more than 23,000 grants to improve facilities to the tune of £877m. These grants paid for 1,000 artificial grass pitches,

11,000 natural grass pitches and 1,300 changing rooms. This has attracted an additional £1.23bn of partnership funding, according to the Foundation, making up more than £2bn of investment in grassroots football.

The only problem is, if you don't own your ground, or have anything other than a long lease, forget it.

'We'll be looking for grants, obviously, there's lots of grants you can get from the FA and lottery and all sorts of different bits and pieces and then the balance obviously, the club, and me,' says Lancaster.

The final say will go to the planners at Wychavon District Council in Droitwich. A few die-hard fans have their doubts.

'Honestly, I think it is unlikely,' says Evans, echoing the views of a number of others in the know that I spoke to.

'But I think we are on the road to a new ground ... The plans are fantastic, it should happen, but it is Wychavon Council, that may be friendlier than Worcester City Council, but you know it is a decision they will make. They should pass it; it is good for the community, it is good for football, it is good for the people, but it is just a plan.'

A few months later I spoke to a long-term Fernhill Heath resident in a shop in Friar Street as she bought a new battery for a timepiece she's owned for half a century. She looked like many who attended the planning show at Fernhill Heath Memorial Hall, but sounded completely different.

'I hope they get it, to be honest, if they can sort out the parking,' she says.

Why?

'They've got nowhere else to go. It would be such a shame if football disappeared from the city.'

Surely, music to the ears of the men struggling to find Worcester City a new home.

If Lancaster and Harrison fail to secure planning permission, a very frustrating and expensive search will likely stretch far into the future.

A search where beggars will certainly not be choosers and even the best laid plans could end up losers.

Chapter 16

Could Be Worse, Take Jude Bellingham's First Club

JUST 20 miles down the road, ground headaches haunted happy days.

On the face of it times couldn't have been better for Jude Bellingham's first club, Stourbridge, but behind the back-slapping and reflected glory this is a club fighting for its very survival.

In the cold light of day, like Worcester City, the club needs money and its own ground more than cheers and reflected glory. Unlike Worcester, Stourbridge has never flirted with bankruptcy, yet, like Worcester, not owning a ground is the biggest threat to its future. All of this was put to the back of the mind, as the Stourbridge-born England star danced his way through Euro 2024. The social club at Amblecote – the home ground of Southern League Stourbridge – was filled for every game.

'He's one of our own!' sang Stourbridge supporters after Bellingham scored England's first goal of the tournament, against Serbia, on the way to the final.

TV crews flocked to Stourbridge for colour stories and live crossings. Some of the supporters appeared on TV more often than Eamonn Holmes, putting the club on the map.

Stourbridge gave Bellingham his first season in football when he was about seven years old.

When he signed for Real Madrid for more than £88 million, the Spanish club used film of the young Bellingham scoring in the red-and-white stripes of Stourbridge. Heavens, in my day reporting at Amblecote for the *County Express*, Stourbridge players were happy for a mention in the *Sports Argus*!

Supporters often joke that Stourbridge should get a development fee from Real Madrid for Bellingham's first year in football. Unlikely.

A picture of Bellingham, standing in the famous Shed stand at the far end of the ground, adorns the wall of the Stourbridge social club. The Shed, a huge green terraced barn behind the far goal, is the source of a good deal of noise in games; the fans call it the 12th man.

It has been partially closed off for a year or so because of subsidence under the back of the stand that'll take tens of thousands of pounds to fix.

Instead of a development fee, maybe Bellingham could donate a day's wages to fix up part of the ground where he kicked his first ball. Perhaps the club could call it the Jude Bellingham stand.

This is the ground where I first saw the infant Bellingham, standing knee high to his mother, watching his father Mark Bellingham play for Stourbridge, when I was on a visit home from Africa about 15 years ago.

Bellingham senior, a police sergeant just down the road in Halesowen, was a remarkable and ruthless goalscorer who knocked in 700 goals in his 20-club career. He was fast and fearsome; with his head down, charging at defenders, he always put me in mind of a bullet from a gun. Non-League defenders didn't know what to do with him and he was worth paying to watch.

The proud father is now retired from the force and manager of his son's multi-million-pound career.

By contrast, the two people who run Stourbridge are trying to figure out how to raise millions to give the club a future.

Andy and Andy, they call them on the terraces at Amblecote. Fourteen years after taking over a struggling club they have restored its reputation as one of the top non-League clubs in the Midlands.

Both are likeable guys from hard-working families, who have lived life.

In many ways they are very much what the times demand. Like Worcester City's Simon Lancaster, they are football men with business minds; Stourbridge boys made good, who believe in the club, watch from the terraces and drink with the fans.

Andy Pountney is the chairman. An outspoken, straight-talking character with a capital 'C'. I remember him supporting the club, vociferously, standing on the side near the players' entrance with his dad in the 1970s. His grandfather was also a Stourbridge supporter.

Pountney has been highly successful in business, allowing him to put a fair amount of his money where his mouth is. He started out as a Youth Training Scheme worker on £25 a week, when he was a teenager, driving forklift trucks in a warehouse a ten-minute drive from the ground.

In 1986, Pountney saved up enough to buy his first Transit van for £800 – he even remembers the registration plate – which changed his life. With it, he delivered Bridgestone tyres all over England and invested in his own business.

Pountney now employs 60 people and turns over millions of pounds with his company Andyfreight.

'Part of my business now is the very warehouse where I started out driving forklifts as a YTS trainee!' he says.

Andy Bullingham was a professional footballer with Nottingham Forest, born-and-bred in Stourbridge. He played for his hometown club on his painful tumble down the football pyramid.

His is a cautionary tale of promise and pain that befalls many a keen young talented footballer in provincial England.

It began in Sunday district football in Stourbridge, where the 13-year-old Bullingham scored for fun.

Word got out and scouts from West Ham, Everton and Manchester United took a look at him.

A father of a team-mate was a scout for Nottingham Forest and took it further. He arranged a meeting with the late, great Brian Clough who had won a League title for the club and two European Cups. At the City Ground, in Nottingham, smiling club officials ushered the teenage Bullingham and his parents into a room with Clough and his right-hand man Peter Taylor.

'This is the best club in the country. Why wouldn't you want to sign for us?' said Clough.

'The next minute Cloughie has his arm around your mother and is shaking your dad's hand and that was that,' recalls

Bullingham. He signed along with Darren Wassall, the son of Kidderminster Harriers legend Brendan, and full-back Brett Williams, from nearby Quarry Bank, who was to play in Clough's last home match in 1993.

Life with Brian was never easy. Bullingham recalls the manager would kiss you on the cheek one day and clip you around the ear the next.

Life wasn't easy for the young hopefuls at Nottingham Forest, full stop. Clough and Taylor used to make them squat down with their backs against the wall; the first player to collapse was given an unpopular chore.

Former Forest goalkeeper Mark Crossley dined out on a story of how he was dragooned into playing for Simon Clough's Sunday league team, the day after a heroic performance in the FA Cup. The league fined the Sunday team for bringing in a ringer and Clough took it out of Crossley's wages.

Bullingham recalls not only being ordered to play football for the manager's son, but also Sunday teams run by his other son, Nigel, and another run by Forest's England international Des Walker.

In the week, the young players were often despatched to dig Mrs Clough's garden.

Time spent with Clough could be unpredictable, to say the least. At an away game at Wimbledon, the 18-year-old Bullingham was sat next to Clough in the stand as a home supporter shouted loudly behind them.

'Cloughie turns round and says: "You can shut your mouth!" Cloughie scared the man to death, he was shaking like a leaf!' says Bullingham.

In the boardroom, at half-time, Clough filled a glass with whiskey and handed it to Bullingham.

'Take it to that bloke and say I am sorry,' said Clough. Bullingham went back up to the stand to find the mouthy supporter had fled.

On the bus home from an away defeat, Clough heard Forest players laughing. He rushed to the back of the bus.

'You think it is funny? Laugh again and you'll fucking walk back.'

Bullingham also roomed with Peter Davenport, the future Manchester United striker, and will never forget the team talk before his first game.

'Clough got all the players to stand in a circle round Davenport and said: "This is the best player in the team, and he can play. So when you get the ball give it to him" ... That was the team talk!'

Then came calamity for Bullingham. A crunching tackle shattered his cruciate ligament. He paid for surgery, but he was never as sharp again.

'I knew I wouldn't play again as a professional, I'd had it,' says Bullingham. He was 19.

'I sat at home doing bugger all. My dad played football with Mac Lycett [a former Stourbridge manager] and he got me to play five games for Stourbridge. I then moved on to Kidderminster, a bigger club in the National League.'

Then came the rapid and humbling tumble down the leagues for the dedicated professional, who had dreamed of playing at Wembley and ended up playing at Cradley.

Eighteen months later he was playing a game in the Dudley and Cradley League, for a few bob, and came up against two old school mates.

'What are you fucking doing?' they said. This existential moment prompted Bullingham to go back to college to study for a B-Tech and train to be an insurance broker.

'I wanted a job with a shirt and tie and decided I ain't wearing overalls,' he says with a smile.

Bullingham founded JPM Insurance, in 2005, and made more than enough money to help keep a football club afloat in his spare time.

Pountney and Bullingham met through the insurance business and both had connections to Stourbridge. In 2010 they sat down over a pint to draw up a five-year business plan for a club living hand-to-mouth.

'At the time this was a tip, it should have been closed down. The changing rooms were awful, the pitch wasn't great,' says Pountney.

'We have seen it with other clubs where people come in with money saying they will invest, but ultimately they drain the club.

We wrote a business plan, based on sustainability and rebuilding the club from the ground up. Wanted it to become a community club,' says Bullingham, who also admits his painful experience as a young player spurred him on towards some kind of catharsis.

'I had connections here at Stourbridge and felt I had a bit of unfinished business in football. I was really disappointed how I was handled when the Forest thing ended. I know now, when you look at clubs now, how they release kids and don't support them,' he says.

'If somebody gets released from a top-flight club, somebody has to put their arm round them and get them back into the system. I'm surprised the impact that had on me. I had a scar in there I needed to deal with it myself. Because it was hurting, so from that perspective, being involved in this club has been brilliant.'

It is also increasingly expensive. The cost of maintaining a decent standard of football goes up every year at a club which turns over £650,000.

Pountney, always with an eye on the books, gives a summary. The club has lost money every year since Covid, but is one of the few in the area which is solvent. It did gather a lot of money in the FA Cup runs between beating Plymouth Argyle in 2011 and losing in the third round to Wycombe Wanderers in 2016; but most of that has been spent on keeping up standards.

'In the close season, the club offered three good players £500 a week. We lost them because someone offered £800 from a league below,' he says in November 2023.

'If we paid that, we would bankrupt the club.'

Stourbridge was paying £1,800 a week in wages in 2010, compared to nearly £5,000 a week in 2024.

'We paid Jason Cowley for a season when he was injured, cost £20,000 in wages. The curse of the contract, we sign someone, and they get injured,' says Pountney.

Promotion to the National League North is likely to prove even more expensive. Aside from the increase in the wage bill, Stourbridge would have to improve the ground, build a new stand and buy better floodlights at an estimated cost of £200,000 – at least!

What about a multi-millionaire saviour? It worked for Wrexham.

'No. Why would he do that? What would he be buying? We don't own the ground,' says Pountney.

'What about selling players?' I ask; always a great lifeline for struggling non-League clubs.

'We had a grand for Jamie Insall from Hibernian. We had the promise of two grand for Devarn Green from Tranmere Rovers, but never got it; £2,000 off Nuneaton for Luke Benbow. We ended up with about £30,000 for Dan Scarr and £12,500 for Ryan Rowe to Kidderminster,' says Pountney.

'I don't think those deals of hundreds of thousands of pounds for a non-League player are there anymore.'

Yet, Andy and Andy plough on season after season, in the face of rising costs and a smattering of criticism.

One of the big costs has been the women's team which has been good enough to win promotion to expensive trips to big clubs like Newcastle and Derby, but has yet to earn the gate money to pay for it. Another source of criticism from some fans.

Vice chairman Bullingham is under no illusions: 'It has become increasingly harder, we talk about this a lot. I think Andy bears the brunt of this, it is nice being vice chairman, I can keep idle. It would be nice to come to games and just watch the football without someone talking to you about the flush not working on the toilets. Volunteers don't exist anymore, but supporters do help with painting, concreting and bricklaying.'

Pountney believes the two, both in their 50s, have a point to prove.

'We've had to work hard, but I do believe there are people at the club who want us to fail. The problem is you are doing it for the benefit of them and it hurts more than somebody slagging off a performance,' he says.

The biggest headache and threat to football at Stourbridge is exactly the same as Worcester City: the club doesn't own its own ground.

This is going to be the biggest and most decisive battle in the club's 150-year history in which the landlords are as much help as a midfielder who can't trap a bag of spuds.

Chapter 17

A Club Clinging to a Cliff

IT COULD have been one of God's little jokes. Millions waved before the eyes in the cause of saving a proud football club from the abyss, then nothing.

The man from the Football Foundation arrived at Stourbridge in the 2023/24 season promising millions of pounds to rebuild Stourbridge's ancient football ground; a dream come true. New stands, new changing rooms, new hope.

The Football Foundation had already handed out millions in Premier League money to other, smaller clubs in the Midlands to help boost grassroots football. It has earmarked Stourbridge as a go-ahead club that it wants to give money to.

Club chairman Andy Pountney remembers the meeting with a twinkle in his eye.

'It is not pie in the sky. They selected us saying "You are doing a fantastic job with the academy and the kids, the disabled, the ladies; what do you want?" I said "We want a new stand down here, a three-quarter size 3G pitch,' which we have already proposed to the council. We had drawings done, sent them to the council two years ago,' says Pountney.

For this to happen would take little short of a miracle. All Stourbridge need to do is persuade a leaden-footed council to extend the club's lease and, hey presto, millions will flow from the Football Foundation.

Or, allow the football club to buy the ground and move the cricket club off to make way for new pitches and stands. This is about as likely as Liz Truss and Joe Biden making a political comeback on the same day.

It all adds up to a giant ground headache that Worcester City, which has plenty of its own problems, can be relieved it does not have. Amblecote, the home of Stourbridge Football Club, sits on top of a shelf of sandstone and cinder banks overlooking the rooftops of the town.

It is a loveable, but odd, football ground, which reflects the industry of the Black Country which paid for it. It looks haphazard and ageing, to put it kindly.

The council, then Stourbridge Corporation, took over the ground in 1921 and granted the first lease.

Not long afterwards, the council built the football club stands, which have changed little 100 years later and Pountney reckons they've cost the club a few signings.

'If you bring in millennials, they want to come in and see this fancy new stadium, new ground and 3G pitch and all that ... to ask a 20-year-old to come here and they see those two old stands ... it is a hard sell.'

The stands perch on a cinder bank near the top of a sheer drop into factory sites. The bank behind the Shed, the stand behind the goal, which draws the noisiest supporters, is showing signs of subsidence and the club has closed half of it pending a five-figure repair bill.

'It is a sandstone bank. If you looked behind the green fence you can see how much it has fallen in the last ten years. It is like coastal erosion,' says former club chairman Ian Pilkington.

Also on the history front, there is a war memorial arch at the entrance to the ground, almost identical to the one at Gheluvelt Park in Worcester. It is Grade II listed, along with the turnstiles, which puts it on par with Battersea Power Station and the Middlesbrough Transporter Bridge.

On one side of the ground there is a cricket pitch and under the centre circle are caverns, long sealed off, which were used as an air raid shelter during World War Two. US soldiers also made camp in the cricket pavilion in the last couple of years of the conflict.

The football club started out in 1876 playing at the back of the Rifleman's Arms, in Wood Street, just over the cliff in nearby Wollaston.

As success swelled the crowds into thousands, the club moved to Amblecote in 1888 to share with the cricket club, which had been playing there since 1857.

The good news is that it is cheap and fairly secure. Dudley Council charges a peppercorn rent for land covenanted for sports and recreation only.

This means, unless there is a major change of use, it should be safe from housing developers or supermarket builders.

But this lease poses a big problem when it comes to attracting Football Foundation millions. You can't get the money unless you have at least a ten-year lease. At the time of writing the club has eight years of a 25-year lease left.

'We need to negotiate now so we can get funding and support to sustain. If we don't get a new lease extending more than ten years, so we can get funding to maintain us, we won't exist anyway,' says Pountney.

'We've got a club on land we don't own, an air raid shelter under the pitch on a ground we can only use eight months of the year.'

The club has put forward its sweeping plan to buy Amblecote. Chairman Pountney outlines the dream.

'We said, sell it to us, give the cricket club Mary Stevens Park – there is a cricket wicket there. We will buy this off you; the money we give you would help support the development of the cricket club. Maybe, £1.2m. Then we went to the members and said we wanted to change the constitution of the club and the way it is run so we can own the freehold to get investors in,' he says.

'So, say it cost you £2m, you can get ten investors putting £200,000 in and then the investors all get ten per cent of the shares ... We took this to the council two years ago and we got knocked back.'

Speaking about being knocked for six, I approached John Huband, the chairman of Stourbridge Cricket Club, to ask him whether the cricketers would move.

'No, no and no,' he replied.

Huband, who played cricket for Stourbridge for 27 years, believes the club has its own illustrious history hosting county cricket and players of the calibre of Richie Benaud, Imran Khan and Kapil Dev.

'It is not going to change. We don't need crowds of three or four thousand to survive. We only pay expenses to a few players. We are run by volunteers on the bar and functions,' says Huband.

"There is no need for us to move. We are 180 years old here. There is no money for anyone to move anywhere. We are not a wealthy club.'

It seems the landlords, Dudley Council, are as immovable as the cricket club.

When I told supporters I was going to approach Dudley Council, they laughed.

'Forget it, Chris,' they said.

But no, my journalistic integrity came first. I started phoning Dudley Council. I left messages with no reply; after a couple of weeks, by chance, I got through to the man in charge on his landline: Steve Cooper, the head of corporate landlord services.

'I am not allowed to talk about our tenants,' he said as if it were a matter of national security. He said he had handed over my questions to the press office and hadn't I heard from them? No.

A few days later, a call from someone called Wayne in the press office saying it would be dealt with. Another month, or so, of nothing. More and more daily calls for weeks and weeks and messages left; nothing. I got another call, this time from a woman in the press office who said my questions would be dealt with swiftly. Nothing.

These are public servants paid good wages to deal with the money and issues of the people.

As my late grandfather would have said: 'I wouldn't pay them in washers!'

'I think something radical will have to happen for the council to take notice. I don't think there is any other way to doing it. They are disaster management people, aren't they? Unless we get a bloody nose, nothing is going to happen,' says Bullingham.

'They won't negotiate with us because of the issue with the banks [subsidence]. Now they're trying to establish where the lease sits regarding the ownership of the land and the bank and who is responsible. We could be waiting ad infinitum.'

The longer the wait, the worse it could be, fear supporters.

'We are talking about a local authority. If nothing changes, they will be so bankrupt they will sell it. Houses are being built all around the ground. You can see what is happening … People think it won't happen; people have to be aware that it is a possibility,' says Pilkington, a supporter for a half a century.

'Until we can get the ground situation sorted out – and I am an old codger now – I am sincerely worried. There will be a Stourbridge team, but will it be playing in the Kidderminster league or somewhere like that? That is the concern,' says Joe Billingham, who has supported Stourbridge since 1962.

The bottom line is the club can't go forward and might end up going backwards, according to Bullingham.

'It is hard doing what we do, knowing we can't go anywhere. If we don't get a decision from the council, we will wrap it all up and just have the first team,' he says.

Football teams shut down after years of investment and building. Hundreds of young dreams crushed in a football retreat; it may not bother Dudley Council, but it scares the hell out of me and surely anyone who cares about non-League football.

Chapter 18

Why Abandon Chelsea for Worcester City

BACK IN Worcester, spring was in the air. The spray of white pear blossom peeped over one of the garden walls, like a long-lost friend, at the back of the grand cluster of houses that line St George's Square in Barbourne on the northern route out of Worcester.

A sign that the city was waking up from the long winter, just like its football club.

Overhead, fast-moving clouds were thick and a little dark, but like Worcester City's opposition on the afternoon of 3 February 2024, they were far from threatening.

Hellenic League whipping boys could have been a name invented for Lydney Town from the Forest of Dean, who had made the 50-mile trip north for yet another beating.

A few months before, in October, when the Worcester City promotion bandwagon headed down the dark and windy country lanes of Gloucestershire, it spelt doom for Lydney Town.

It is a fair journey from Worcester; a fair distance from decent mobile phone reception, I can tell you, along the banks of the beautiful Severn Estuary towards Swan Road, the home of 114-year-old Lydney Town.

Swan Road may have a capacity of 700 but appears unlikely to reach it any time soon.

Not that many home supporters are keen to amble down the dark and narrow lane from the town to watch their losing team.

On the night of the Worcester City game, it was a good attendance. The man taking money on the main gate had surprise written all over his face as around 150 unfamiliar faces from Worcestershire rolled through in the ten minutes before kick-off; he looked a bit like a father at his teenage daughter's birthday party who didn't realise she had so many friends. The crowd was a mere 227.

Worcester City weren't there to make friends on the night, starting with a free kick like a bullet from City defender Adam Mace early in the first half. There was so much power in the shot that the Lydney keeper almost threw it in the net like it was a hot cannonball.

It was a special night for City's Dylan Hart, signed from Bewdley Town in the dark days of the previous season. He repaid his manager's faith with a hat-trick on his first start of the season.

The last goal of the hat-trick was a picture. A furious dash down the right and a shot lashed across the goal into the far corner. Hart raised his arms in triumph, a couple of yards in front of me, and quite right too.

Worcester City coach Chris Cornes told the *Worcester News*: 'The fans haven't seen the best of him yet and I know he's been working hard in the off-season to come back fitter and stronger. I'm hoping he hits the ground running and scores the goals we need to compete in this league.'

Hart responded: 'The season was stop-start from my point of view but I'm hoping this season I can show the faithful what I'm really about. I can't wait to get started and give them something to celebrate. The decision was a no-brainer, thanks to the incredible support I received last season from our fans.'

By the time Lydney Town arrived in Worcester, four months later, the team was second from bottom having shipped a basinful of goals. The club hadn't won for seven games.

Hart may have been on the sidelines for this game, but there were plenty of other players fighting to get on the scoresheet.

Many of Lydney's players turn out for nothing; the better players merely get expenses to entertain a hardcore of around 40 spectators at home.

No amount of money would have compensated for the thrashing that in-form Worcester City meted out on this mild February afternoon before nearly 700 fans.

Worcester City and non-League football in general have benefitted at the turnstiles from fans being priced out of the increasingly distant moneybags Premier League and Championship.

On this afternoon I spoke to a Queens Park Rangers supporter with his two young sons. He had moved north to work in Worcester.

'There is no way I could afford to take my sons to watch QPR. Now we prefer to watch grassroots football,' he says.

Another supporter, a retired horticulturalist, drives from Wolverhampton for home games and to away games across Gloucestershire and Wiltshire. He held a season ticket for Chelsea for nearly 50 years, but now he has given it up.

'There is too much money slushing around the Premier League. I can't relate to the players anymore. At least non-League football is real,' he says.

'And the away games are good, you can always make a day of it!'

'Just can't stand VAR,' says another former Wolverhampton Wanderers supporter more bluntly.

'A lot of fans who used to go to Wolves and West Brom come to Worcester now because you can touch the players, you can touch the manager and everybody looks after each other; it is a massive difference,' says Richard Widdowson, of the Supporters' Trust, who films every game for Worcester City TV.

Widdowson's lens was fixed on the visitors from Lydney on this day. From the kick-off, the home team blossomed with the pear trees.

City were two up within minutes and 4-0 up by the break. The City forwards waltzed through the Lydney defenders like they were statues.

The pick of the first-half strikes was the fourth by the diminutive dynamo Elliot Hartley.

A powerful and determined run to the byline by right-back Logan Stoddart, followed by a pinpoint cross to Hartley, just outside the penalty area on the right.

Hartley swept the ball into the corner of the Lydney net with such panache and precision that all that was missing was a quick pirouette. Instead, he high-fived a couple of young supporters behind the goal.

Many, including me, thought that Hartley, another survivor of the disastrous previous season, wasn't strong enough to survive at this level.

In this first game of February, after months of brave play, Hartley confirmed we were all wrong and he won the man-of-the-match award.

It would have been double figures before half-time if it hadn't been for the brave and agile Lydney keeper Richard Thomas. The former Bristol City gloveman made double-save, after double-save.

At half-time, the talk over pints of beer behind the goal turned to new owner Simon Lancaster, the future of the club and Wembley.

The following week, Worcester City were to play nearby rivals Stourport Swifts for a place in the FA Vase quarter-final.

'We need someone like Lancaster. Not some big shot who is going to just pour money in and ruin the club. At least he has a plan to bring the club up slowly, step by step. That is what we need,' says a fan who has been following Worcester City since the 1960s.

Talk quickly turned to the prospect of a new ground; in the month public consultation was to begin for the proposal for the Worcestershire Sports Park at Fernhill Heath, just down the road from Claines Lane.

'New ground? But we've got no planning permission. What is the point of making announcements when there is nothing behind it?'

Another fan says the club should think carefully before getting too carried away with the 700 and 800 crowds Worcester City is drawing for the weekly thrashing of small fry like Lydney Town.

'When we get promoted and maybe struggle against better sides, next season you could see this crowd go back to the hardcore of 200, like it was in the bad old days.'

But dreams of Wembley and the FA Vase final melted terrace cynicism.

'Worcester City at Wembley! What price that?' says one of the elders.

I venture that 10,000, maybe 15,000, may make the journey from Worcester to London.

'And the rest,' says the elder.

'You can be sure the Mayor of Worcester, and the councillors will be first on the coach! Doesn't want to help us when we need a new ground, but he'll be the first to grab the glory. Well, he's not coming on my coach!'

The whistle for the second half halted this stream of consciousness and opened the way to two more goals. It seemed nothing could stop Worcester City from climbing back to the top of the table.

Equal on points with title rivals Corsham, but with a far superior goal difference and four games in hand.

It wasn't much of a contest, boys against men, really. Yet, entertaining if you merely wanted to see Worcester City victorious in a comprehensive demolition of the opposition.

The lean and leaping Kyle Belmonte headed home the fifth at the far post on 65 minutes. Worcester born-and-bred Jamie Insall scrambled home the sixth after the keeper had parried. He did his strange goal celebration of robotic moves followed by a low bow that could have come from the court of Henry VIII.

By the final whistle it was 6-0. It could have easily been eight or nine. You got the feeling that the Lydney players were merely trying to keep the score in single figures in the last half an hour.

Not surprisingly, the Lydney keeper Thomas looked dejected as he trudged off at the end. He had played a blinder for 90 minutes and still saw six goals fly past him thanks, largely, to his leaden-footed defenders. There must be a better way to earn a few bob in expenses on a Saturday than diving in the mud parrying bullet shots flying in from every angle.

That is non-League football, you could have told him, but in the dark of this cool afternoon he surely didn't want to hear it.

The bus back into the city, along the Droitwich Road, was full to bursting with optimism and City fans as it ground back into the dark of the city-centre streets.

Most were pensioners feeling the pace of a long afternoon. Many had feasted well at the bar as well as on victory on the pitch.

'Oh, I don't think I will manage to stay awake until the end of *Vera* tonight,' says the man sat next to me to his friend standing in the aisle.

'I will be alright, I'm going to watch *Inspector Morse!*'

Another Saturday night in Worcester.

Chapter 19

The Path to Wembley is Rarely Smooth

THE NEXT stretch of the road to Wembley for Worcester City led across Stourport Bridge over the swollen River Severn. It was an hour before kick-off and already heavy-set, middle-aged men were wobbling out of pubs to make their way across the long iron bridge to Walshes Meadow, the home of Stourport Swifts, the next team standing in the way of Worcester's Wembley dream. The club had already beaten Sleaford Town 2-0 in the first round, Wolverhampton Casuals 3-1 away in the second and Boston at home 2-0 in the third round and 2-0 over Lichfield City in the fourth.

After heavy rain, there were doubts, that the game would even be played, but the sun smiled on Stourport with a welcome drying wind.

The elders were joined by groups of younger lads, walking a lot faster, with sharp, trimmed beards you could have cut your finger on.

I had purposely walked a long way across the town of my birth in tribute to an old college friend and Worcester City fan who had died a few days before. He was a fitness fanatic and marathon runner who sadly collapsed and died in St John's, as he ran home from work. Forty-four years before, one of my oldest friends pointed out the long-haired Graham Plumpton in the college refectory, at Worcester Technical College, where I studied English law, English literature and economics.

'See him, he is a huge Worcester City fan,' says my mate.

It was 1979 and the first season of the Alliance Premier League and I admired how Graham followed City everywhere and talked excitedly about it – a bundle of energy; from a day trip to Bangor, to a shit show in Salisbury where they got kicked unceremoniously out of the FA Cup by a last-minute goal.

Months later, Graham, a group of friends from the Tech, and myself walked to St George's Lane for the Worcestershire Senior Cup Final against Kidderminster Harriers in April 1980. Barry Williams, Barry Lowe and Kenny Lawrence and co were ready to tear up their rivals from 14 miles up the A449.

We stood on the terracing in front of the Brookside Stand in the spring sunshine and laughed and joked throughout the whole 90 minutes, as Worcester City easily despatched Kidderminster Harriers thanks to a Gerry O'Hara goal.

We were 17 years old and didn't have a care in the world. In my mind's eye I can still see Graham and the lads creasing up with laughter. Precious joyful hours of freedom and friendship; in our youth, on days like that, anything in life seemed possible.

I was thinking of super-fit Graham as we walked across the bridge with about 100 City fans. One of them turned and held his sides in pain.

'I am absolutely knackered,' says the man fresh from the pub, about the same age as Graham, as he paused for a breather. 'I have never walked so far to a football match in my life!'

This wasn't just any match. This was an historic fifth-round FA Vase tie with Stourport Swifts. Both sides stood just three games from Wembley; for the Swifts this was a big day out even though they were at home.

Walshes Meadow hasn't changed that much in the 50 years since I first kicked a ball around it as a schoolkid. A small stand has been built on one side and the barriers around the ground have been improved.

On the river side, green-fingered Swifts volunteers have grown a row of huge trees big enough to cover half the pitch if they ever fell down.

The trees are supposed to stop stray balls ending up in the River Severn. Strangely, when a player blasted a ball in that direction they seemed to burst through the trees never to be seen again. Certainly no one bothered to rush to retrieve them, so you wonder what happens to them.

Many of my schoolfriends pulled on the black and gold to play on this pitch for the Swifts, back in the day. Like the club itself, very few of them got very far in the game.

Then again, we went to Stourport High School on the far side of the river, a respectable language college now, but, in my day, it was a violent pit of ignorance.

How I emerged from that school with six O-Levels on my way to becoming a well-travelled journalist, author and writer, who reported from all continents, is one of the wonders of the world.

'It was a horrible school,' said one of my former teachers when I met him many years later. I couldn't help but agree. If you wanted to avoid bruises, it was the kind of school where you had to pretend you were thick during lessons and work like a demon on your homework. At least, that is how I did it.

As Walshes Meadow filled up, on this cool February afternoon, history was in the air.

This was to be the biggest crowd in the 142-year history of Stourport Swifts; a sold-out 1,900 crowd. That is the equivalent of nearly a tenth of Stourport's 20,000 population.

Around 1,600 of the crowd were from Worcester and they filled up nearly three sides of the tiny ground; they drank and ate pizza as if they owned the place as kick-off beckoned.

It didn't take City long to also assert dominance on the pitch. A disallowed goal, then minutes later Kirk Layton put City 1-0 up.

Jamie Insall scored the second for City with a flicked header and celebrated with his robotic moves followed by his trademark Earl of Essex-style low bow. The Stourport fans showered him with insults and beer.

By half-time, City were on fire.

In the final third, as they say on TV, Insall was flicking balls on for fun, bamboozling the Stourport defence and opening up gaping spaces for his fellow attackers. The Stourport defenders didn't know whether it was Saturday or Sunday. Insall, in his final season as a player, was as influential in the team as anyone.

'He's different,' says team-mate Izak Reid, laughing. 'That's a nice way of putting it, yeah, he's a good lad to be fair.'

'If you're going to war, or something like that, he's the first person you'd want with you, he'd back you to the hilt.'

The best was yet to come. One Insall flick fell to the feet of striker Kyle Belmonte about 25 yards from goal. How many attackers at this level would have blasted the chance over the top?

Belmonte spotted the keeper a couple of yards off his line, took a touch, then chipped deftly over the keeper's head into the back of the net. Inch perfect; it was like it all happened in slow motion. He ran over to the packed Stourport fans – probably not the most diplomatic of moves – and was also showered with beer.

On social media, Belmonte, a teetotaller, joked that he couldn't believe how people could throw beer when it was £5 a pint.

'Of all non-League footballers I watch he is my favourite. Sometimes he will run full pelt at somebody and go for the wild challenge, which we haven't seen that much of this season,' says journalist Marcello Cossali-Francis.

'He is just an all or nothing type player, he enjoys playing football, he enjoys being part of a team. He is always posting on social media, not too shy for anything and always plays with a massive smile on his face. But he is crackers, he wouldn't mind me saying that he is bat-shit crazy and a brilliant bloke; he is always laughing on and off the pitch. At the end of the day, he is a brilliant, brilliant, player.'

Joking apart, I find it disgusting when supposed mature adults throw beer in the face of athletes. I see it as an insult to our game, an insult to our sons.

Maybe I'm just old fashioned; but worse was to come as the game wore on.

On the pitch, City were a joy to behold in the second half. Two beautiful one-touch exchanges criss-crossed the pitch, punctuated by Insall's sweet touches. They yielded two goals by Belmonte and the terror of the wing Liam Lockett, who slid in for the fifth that gloriously seemed to take forever to crawl over the line.

Then it turned ugly. Far too many pints went down people's throats on this afternoon, as well as into players' faces. On either side of the flimsy temporary barriers, dividing the Stourport and Worcester fans, pathetic drunken anger grew. To make matters worse, goading poured petrol on the fire.

'You're just a town full of gyppos!' sang the Worcester fans to the fury of Stourport supporters in their smart new black-

and-gold scarves; surely, everyone was old enough to know better, but no.

'The wheels on your house go round and round,' the Worcester fans kept on, 'Where's your caravan?'

'Hey, stop tarmacking my nan's drive!' shouted a young clean-cut man behind the goal with a beer in hand.

OK, there was a lot of sniggering on both sides of the fence, but it all struck me as unnecessary banter likely to create trouble.

On the other side of the fence, young men, probably the grandchildren of people I went to school with, were sitting on the shoulders of their elders chanting rubbish back. There was much pathetic, playground posturing close to the steel fence.

In the confusion, a young man from the Stourport side of the fence strolled around it and launched a clumsy attack on a City fan. All of a sudden two men old enough to know better rolled on the floor in embarrassing unarmed combat. Really?

As I left the ground, the police had arrived and at last formed a line separating the bickering fans. The ugliest was saved for last.

I saw a man on the Worcester side of the fence scratching his armpits, shaking his legs and making monkey noises at the Stourport supporters. Can you believe it in the 21st century? Disgusting: shouldn't this kind of rubbish be left in the bin with the racist banana-throwing thuggery of the 1970s?

A police investigation was launched soon after the game. Overall, a day that should have been full of civic pride and history degenerated into an ugly exchange tainted with shame.

The trouble at the game made headlines that Worcester City didn't need as the club prepared to apply for planning permission for a new stadium on the grounds that the fans won't be a problem. It probably didn't have that much effect at the end of the day.

Club sponsor Tim Evans was at Stourport and was unfazed by this pungent whiff of trouble off the pitch.

'That is a very isolated case. I have never ever seen trouble at a Worcester City game. I've seen Cheltenham fans coming in to stir trouble when we played Gloucester and we had one copper, but I have never seen any real trouble,' says Evans.

'When you think there was nearly 2,000 people there and you look at the isolated trouble there was there. That wouldn't have happened at Worcester City. When you have got a small club like Stourport with an attendance way in excess of what they are used to, I think they got caught out a bit. At Worcester we would not have been caught out because we have people there who are used to big attendances. It is isolated and it is the wrong headline, but everything has a knock-on effect.'

On the brighter side of an historic day, Worcester City earned a good draw for the quarter-final. Victory in that game, in March, would mean a two-legged semi-final and possibly Wembley for the first time in City's 122-year history.

The draw was Emley AFC, a village team just outside Huddersfield in Yorkshire, at home. The Yorkshire club made the long, daunting, trip south to face a rampant Worcester City. Emley had beaten fancied Whickham 2-0 in the previous round and had been FA Vase finalists at Wembley back in 1988, losing 1-0 to Colne Dynamos. The Yorkshire team was also on a run of nine wins.

To put it all into perspective, Worcester City took more fans to Stourport Swifts than the entire population of the village of Emley.

It promised to be a tough away game for the villagers. On the other hand, Goliath never beat David, did he?

On the day, 8 March, Goliath kicked David's arse into the middle of next week, so to speak.

Worcester City didn't so much beat Emley, as steamroller them.

Winger Liam Lockett got the first with a pile-driver over the goalkeeper's head in the 22nd minute, followed by another neat finish in the 75th minute.

Emley chipped in with an own goal on what was to prove a miserable afternoon for the Yorkshiremen. The visitors fought hard to get back into the game in the second half, but it appeared beyond them.

Izak Reid, an electrician by trade, skipped through the defence to make it 4-0 to Worcester City in injury time. It was a record 15th consecutive win for the club.

The Worcester City players celebrated with the fans and there was a team photograph at the final whistle – all that was missing from the pictures was a trophy.

Ahead of Worcester City, stood a two-legged semi-final with Great Wakering Rovers from near Southend.

The Essex club was formed in 1919 by demobilised soldiers from the First World War who worked at a nearby brickworks. Like the reborn Worcester City, it is a club built on love and volunteer labour.

Farmer and supporter Roger Burroughs helped secure a lease on former allotments from the parish council in 1985.

With their bare hands, volunteers built the ground brick by brick and named it Burroughs Park, in his honour.

Success was not so easy to build in this season. Great Wakering Rovers were halfway down the Essex Senior League in March 2024 alongside Athletic Newham FC, Frenford and Coggeshall FC. Who? Exactly.

The Essex David, having seen the thrashing handed out to the Yorkshire version, must have taken a deep breath before he brought his slingshot and bag of stones to Worcester, in April, for the first leg of the semi-final at the former Worcester Warriors stadium at Sixways.

Chapter 20

Nobby and his Sprinkle of Bone-Dust Magic

SPEAKING OF the glory days of Worcester City.

If there was one character dominating the glory days of Worcester City it was a flamboyant, larger-than-life Brummie plumber by the name of Nobby Clark.

You could argue Clark and Worcester City were made for each other. He joined City in December 1974 when the club was at a low ebb, with an even lower bank balance, following relegation the season before.

In these dark times, Worcester City were fortunate to team up with a remarkable manager. Clark had charisma and chutzpah to burn.

When Worcester City prepared to play top-flight Coventry City, in the FA Cup in 1983, a television interviewer asked Clark earnestly what he was going to say to his players before the game.

'All play the same way lads,' said Clark with a glint in his eye.

Despite this relish for the job, it took three weeks for Clark to decide to take up the reins of his first wage-paying club. He had fallen into full-time football management almost by mistake.

Clark started off managing his local side Hall Green, in the South Birmingham Premier League, followed by a spell as assistant manager at Darlaston.

Clark moved up to the manager's job at Highgate United, where he took the team to FA Amateur glory and caught the eye of success-starved Worcester City directors.

Clark, who owned a plumbing business in Birmingham, had little money to play with at St George's Lane and a legend to follow. His predecessor Ronnie Radford, the Hereford United hero who humbled Newcastle United with a screamer in the FA Cup a couple of years before, had stepped down after the board forced him to unload long-serving players to cut costs.

By contrast, this penury helped the new manager Clark hone his wheeler-dealer skills in the transfer market.

It was Clark who organised a whip-round in the social club, under the main stand at St George's Lane, to raise £500 to sign mercurial striker Roger Shaw from Redditch United, in December 1976. Clark put in the first bundle of notes from his own pocket.

OK, to the modern fan it is a signing that lacks glory and money; to Worcester City, this was a signing of sheer flair and instinct, worth every penny. It also captures the powerful spirit of volunteerism that runs through the club to this day.

The fruit of this faith was a joy to behold. Shaw veered from conjuring chances out of thin air, to apathy; you simply never knew what he was going to do. The fans called him 'Mr Magic'.

Before one game at St George's Lane, Shaw heard one of the directors say he should have been dropped. Shaw scored a few minutes into the game and ran over to the director's box in the main stand to stick up two defiant fingers to the director who had dared suggest he be left out.

My schoolfriends related the tale, with a laugh, in the playground on Monday; I wish I had seen it. In this uptight day and age, Shaw would have been banned for a few games, at least.

In short, Shaw was not a well-drilled robot, which you see so often these days. He played from the heart; he was a cavalier in boots, whom you would pay to watch. He'd score from an impossible angle, and he'd miss from two yards. He scored 49 goals in 86 games and was reckoned to be one of the best strikers ever to play for Worcester City. It was a sad day when Shaw went back to ply his trade with Redditch United in 1978.

This flair for recruitment helped push the pace as Clark oversaw the glorious run of league title wins and cup runs in the 1970s and early 1980s.

It was nearly ten golden years under Clark. A shoestring budget assembled the most celebrated Worcester City team in history, arguably the most feared non-League side in the land.

Most fans of that era can reel off the names: Malcolm Phelps; Kenny Lawrence; Jimmy Williams; Jim Cumbes; Barry Williams; Kevin Tudor; Gary Stevens; Ralph Puncheon ... and John Barton, who, under Clark's eye, became the most expensive non-League player of his day.

In 1978, Everton paid Worcester City £30,000 for Barton, a record at a time when top-flight players were still selling for six-figure fees. In that year, Gordon McQueen broke the transfer record with a £500,000 move from Leeds United to Manchester United.

The joke at the time was not even Steve McQueen would have cost that much; in 2024, £500,000 is a week's pay for many Premier League stars.

In those days, a non-League club getting anywhere near £30,000 for a defender was about as likely as one of your players landing on the moon.

Forty-six years later Barton is still working in football; as we speak in May 2024, he is about to fly to Croatia with a squad of England's teenage international players. His job is to ensure the young players carry on their studies in the national curriculum while they are away on international duty.

'Worcester City is my club. Always has been, always will be. I played 145 times for Worcester City and scored seven goals. I was proud to manage my club for six years,' he tells me.

Homage from a key member of a team brought together by Clark's keen eye for talent and acumen when it came to bending the rules of the day, which allowed you to put in seven-day notice of an approach for a player.

'Nobby Clark always took advantage of the seven-day rule ... He could find players and talked to everyone about their ability,' says Barton with a smile.

'He could turn the team around in seven days. Even though he wasn't a tracksuit manager, he would listen to the players on who is a good player where, what club. You'd turn up at training next week and that player would be sitting next to you in the dressing room.

What helped managers like Clark, in the 1970s, was that most players were not on contract, merely appearance money.

'He just used to go out and get them because he wouldn't have to deal with contracts in those days and of course once that started, that was the start of the surge of contracts for players in the non-League level.'

Barton admired Clark and was arguably one of the closest players to him at St George's Lane. Like Clark, Barton was a Brummie who fell in love with Worcester and its football club. He too took the road less travelled to professional football.

For a man who played in the top flight and in Europe, Barton has that wonderful old-fashioned quality of humility as he tells how his career began on the bottom rung of non-League football. He admits he couldn't even get in the first team at Aldridge Grammar School.

Like Clark, Barton, one of the most sure-footed defenders of his day, almost stumbled into professional football; one of the great functions that non-League football plays: a net to scoop up lost talent.

It all started on the playing fields of Birmingham. The coach of Boldmere St Michaels, in nearby Sutton Coldfield, contacted Barton at his home in Great Barr. He said he was desperate for players for a Saturday game.

Barton wasn't interested. He was bent on going to watch his beloved Aston Villa, along with 30,000 others at Villa Park, in a top-of-the-table clash in the Third Division, against Bournemouth.

'It all started with my mum. She said to me, "Why don't you just go and help him, he'll be short of players for Saturday," and I said, "No, I'm not going." Ma said I ought to reconsider, and she kept on at me for two days. I thought, "OK, to stop her moaning at me I will go."'

Instead of his planned pilgrimage to Villa Park, Barton took up his boots and journeyed to Church Road, the home of Boldmere St Michaels.

'I had no clue where I was going. I walked to the dressing room, pushed the door and I couldn't open it. I pushed it again and it opened slightly and then somebody opened the door. The reason the door wouldn't open is because they had about 30 players in there! The manager said, "Come on in, John," and I said, "I thought you had no players." He said,"yeah, we're OK, but you're playing!" I said, "You've conned me," and I never went to Villa Park after that.'

Barton learned his trade and moved on to Paget Rangers and Sutton Coldfield Town, before going to ambitious Southern League club Stourbridge where he cut his teeth as a swift marauding right-back. Believe it or not, in those days the Southern League teams were seen as the aristocrats of non-League football.

'I think somebody has got to think you're good enough, but you've also got to be lucky enough as well, and I was,' says Barton about his rapid rise in the game.

Stourbridge was a club flushed with success in 1974; winning promotion to the Premier Division, for the first time. The club also reached the two-legged Welsh Cup Final against Cardiff City and topped it off with an invite to play in an international tournament in Gibraltar. In those days English teams were allowed to enter the Welsh Cup, even though they weren't allowed to take up a European place if they won it.Nearly 6,000 people squeezed into Amblecote to watch Stourbridge take on Cardiff City, any way they could. The current chairman of Stourbridge Andy Pountney recalls watching the final, as an eight-year-old, sitting behind the goal on an old settee.

Stourbridge was also the kingdom of Allan Grundy who, like Clark of Worcester City , was a canny and charismatic coach; another talented reader of the non-League game.

'I thought, "Bloody hell, oh bloody hell, how am I going to get in this team now?" recalls Barton.

Allan Grundy showed some faith in me, I really learnt a lot from those experienced players.'

Grundy, who worked in advertising in Birmingham, was one of those thoughtful coaches of his time, who gave up his nights and weekends to earn a few quid on the side.

In the 21st century, a coach like Grundy, or Clark for that matter, would have been picked up for a well-paid full-time post by the huge technical coaching structure of the modern professional game.

Barton recalls the coaching acumen of Grundy in his Stourbridge days.

'One day, he phoned me up at home in Great Barr, in Birmingham, and said he would meet me at Red House Park and told me to bring my boots. We walked through technical exercises that helped me improve my game. He was like that, he could see stuff in your game and knew how you could improve,' says Barton.

'Graham Allner [a former Stourbridge player who also managed Worcester City and Kidderminster Harriers] learned a lot from Grundy and passed it on to the next generation of players. He could see things in players that few coaches could.'

Barton improved leaps and bounds on the right side of defence at Stourbridge and caught the eye of Worcester City boss Clark. His last game for Stourbridge, which I saw at Villa Park along with 800 others, was against Worcester City in the final of the Birmingham Senior Cup in April 1976.

Worcester City won 1-0, to lift the cup, thanks to a late goal from all-time record scorer John Inglis at the Holte End. The proposed move for Stourbridge's right-back to Worcester City brought the young defender into contact with Clark's door tapping long before the seven-day notice of approach was up.

'Nobby sent a chap named Wyn Bowen, who used to manage at Alvechurch, round to our house to knock on the door. He said I want you to come to Worcester City, and it was just a blur really from Stourbridge. I didn't really know if they were breaking the etiquette of tapping players; they probably were at the time. If they wanted you to go to them, people would be knocking at your door, it was the old Peter Taylor tricks where Cloughy and he would go and knock the door down; it was just a magical time.'

It wasn't always magical for clubs on the receiving end, according to Peter Fryar, a life member and former director of Kidderminster Harriers.

One night sometime in the late 1970s, Clark was in the Kidderminster Harriers Social Club, next to the stadium at Aggborough. According to Fryar, Clark told his hosts he had dropped in for a drink on his way to see a match somewhere.

The hot property at Kidderminster Harriers at the time was John Griffiths, a creative midfielder worth the entrance fee alone.

I can't look at a picture of the diminutive golden-haired Griffiths, who flashed across the pitch in a blur of red and white on Saturdays, without hearing the shout from the terraces at Kidderminster, back in the day: 'Skin 'im, Griffo!'

For that is what Griffiths spent his Saturday afternoons doing. He could twist and turn, always trying something new and bamboozling defenders twice his size. He was the first player at non-League level I ever saw put his foot on the ball, wait for the defender to come, beat him, then show him the ball and beat him again. He was a joy to behold.

For a young, slight, footballing teenager like me he was also an inspiration. In the 1970s, it was all about being tall, big and strong. I once met Griffiths, when my journalist father interviewed his team-mate John Chambers after a game at Aggborough.

Griffiths stood to the right, pulling hard on a cigarette and looking at the floor in what seemed to be a bit of awkward embarrassment. To my shock, he smoked! In a bigger shock I found out I was taller than him! My first lesson in football and life that size doesn't really matter. You can skin anyone if you move quickly and cleverly enough with the ball.

As you can imagine, in that era of laxity regarding fouls, the wrath of these giant slow-footed defenders came down in flying boots. How they didn't manage to cripple Griffiths for life in those violent days beats me.

Again, he was an inspiration on the pitch and a number of clubs, including Clark's Worcester City, wanted to sign him badly.

Griffiths was born in 1951, in Oldbury, on the northern tip of Worcestershire, not too far from West Bromwich Albion. He made his mark with Oldbury and West Smethwick Schools, then Midlands Schoolboys, before Aston Villa signed him as an apprentice. He struggled to break into the first team and after only three appearances, Stockport County signed him.

At Edgeley Park, Griffiths enjoyed an illustrious career, scoring 31 goals in 201 games.

In 1975, he signed for Kidderminster Harriers, where he ruled the midfield roost for another five years. This is one of the strengths of non-League football; talents missed by the big clubs flourish to the joy of the people who support the grassroots game.

The story goes, in the Harriers social club, when the highly rated Griffiths went to the toilet, Clark followed him. The raconteur and club director Fryar, who was having a pint in the bar, picks up the story.

'All of a sudden a long-term supporter of ours came out the toilets and said, "Hey, that effing Nobby Clark is in the toilets tapping up John Griffiths. He's offering him a signing-on fee of £200 and £600 a week!"' recalls Fryar with a laugh.

'That was tremendous money then. Anyway he went off and eventually Nobby came out. Colin Youngjohns [a Harriers director] said, "Hey, Nobby!" He says, "What do you want?"

'Colin says to him, "When you are tapping up our players illegally please check that all the toilets are empty." Nobby said, "I wasn't tapping up the player, he was wanting to hire my caravan for a few weeks.'

'Colin said: "I know it ain't bloody true because you haven't got a caravan!"'

The upshot of this was Worcester City never signed Griffiths, nor went near him after that incident.

By contrast, Barton didn't need Clark to ask him twice to move from Stourbridge to Worcester City.

When he was a young boy, his family used to take the long journey from Birmingham – it was before the M5 was built – to visit relatives. Those days it was like going to the ends of the earth. It so happened these relatives lived near St George's Lane.

One night, in the 1960s, the whole family went to watch Worcester City from the terraces.

Barton was taken by the bright floodlights of St George's Lane and the passion of the supporters. It felt like a professional, big-city club, with more than 4,000 fans on the terraces.

On the pitch, Barton's predecessor at right-back, George Bassett, ran the legs off the opposition all night. It left a lasting impression on the youngster from Birmingham.

'I always remember thinking that night, if I could play just one game for Worcester City, I would be happy,' he recalls.

It turned out Barton was destined to play 145 times for Worcester City in happy times for the club.

Clark persuaded him to sign for £25 a week, in 1976, better money than he was on at Stourbridge. Not much, even by today's standards, but Clark was a good man-manager who knew how to motivate.

'If we were having a good run, he would walk into the dressing room with £50 in cash and hand it over and tell us to share it among ourselves. We would get a few quid each! He used to call it "bone dust", instead of bonus.'

It was all part of putting flesh on the bones of a great team. The stage was set for one of the greatest seasons in the club's history.

Chapter 21

City v Manchester United –
What could have been on nights
of fire and ice

WORCESTER CITY v Manchester United in the FA Cup? It could have happened, oh so easily, in that purple patch of the 1978/79 season.

Our team was probably good enough. All it needed was grit, courage and a bit of luck.

Worcester City had plenty of the first two attributes in the FA Cup in 1978, but, sadly, ran out of the third.

The country needed a sprinkle of magic in November 1978; it was cold, it was miserable and riven by industrial strife. This was the so-called Winter of Discontent when disputes cropped up like weeds. Earlier in November, there had been bread rationing because of a bakers' strike; everyone from car workers to dustbin men downed tools.

For Worcester City, this grim winter was lit up by the first round proper of the FA Cup in November 1978. It was the first time Worcester City had got that far since fans wore the Tony Curtis quiff back in 1960.

It had taken City six games to get there; nine hours of football, including replays against Nobby Clark's old club Highgate United and Bath City.

The replay against minnows Highgate United saw a gate of nearly 2,000 in Worcester. The replay in the fourth qualifying round drew 5,543 people to St George's Lane to see a narrow 2-1 win over Bath City. Can you believe the Football Association scrapped FA Cup replays? Madness.

149

It set up a David-and-Goliath contest at St George's Lane on 25 November 1978, pitting Southern League Worcester City against Plymouth Argyle of the then Third Division of the English Football League; the present-day League One.

Forget about Goliath: this game was more about Nobby v Big Mal.

A hard-working Brummie plumber you could picture taking his children to the park against a flamboyant, champagne-quaffing, cigar-smoking, fedora-wearing playboy manager.

In reality, the difference in wages between Clark and Allison probably wasn't that much in those days. The major difference was Big Mal drinking champagne in the bath versus a pint of bitter for 25p in the Dear's Leap, on the Droitwich Road, supped by the Worcester City players.

I remember many fans couldn't believe that someone they'd seen on TV and read so much about in the newspapers was on his way to St George's Lane. A few couldn't wait to give him a good old-fashioned Worcestershire earful in the stands.

The managers were like chalk and cheese. Clark's world was scouring freezing cold non-League pitches looking for cheap football talent.

By contrast, Allison was one of the first managers to have a lucrative celebrity newspaper column and copious photo splashes in the tabloids, including a picture, taken in the team bath at Crystal Palace, with model Fiona Richmond.

There is no doubt Allison possessed a rare and sharp football brain. England's World Cup-winning captain Bobby Moore said Allison helped turn him into a world-class defender; in more recent times Jose Mourinho claimed Big Mal taught him to be a coach.

Yet, there was another side to his swaggering public persona. When Allison died in 2010, many obituaries referred to him being insecure and filled with self-doubt.

There was no sign of insecurity in the build-up to the game. Allison weighed in with predictions of an easy win in Worcester, as City right-back John Barton recalls.

'Oh yeah, it was all bravado; this that and the other and there was a little bit of setup banter before,' he says.

Many non-League fans across Worcestershire agreed that professional Plymouth Argyle, a team which had never lost to a semi-professional side, would probably prevail.

On the other hand, Worcester City had lost only once in 27 games, to Redditch a week before the Plymouth game.

Clark aced the pre-match mind games. He sent scouts to watch Plymouth Argyle play Lincoln City to assess their goalkeeper and centre-half.

'They're like Dracula, they don't like crosses!' trumpeted the *Worcester Evening News* back-page headline in the week before the game.

Clark had another psychological advantage over Allison. He was going to be in the dugout for the game; while Allison sat it out in the stands.

Inexplicably, Allison was serving his 11th year of a touchline ban for something he said to a linesman in a Manchester City game against Southampton, back in 1968. By the time of the game in Worcester he had appealed three times, unsuccessfully, and sat under his fedora in the stands.

It didn't seem to matter to the Worcester players, as Barton recalls. Thousands of supporters roared the team out on to the pitch. The official attendance was 8,253, but then again, as in many big games at City and elsewhere, you didn't really know as cash came over the turnstiles and disappeared into thin air.

'Worcester's slush fund was the Canal End turnstile. They only opened the Canal End turnstile on big matches and Fulby [club secretary Peter Fulbrook] would take the cash,' says former Kidderminster Harriers director Peter Fryar.

Fulbrook, a fellow journalist who wore bottle-thick glasses, was one of the characters of Midlands non-League football. He was born in Kent and grew up in Wales, after his family were evacuated during the war.

In the 1950s, Fulbrook's father, a policeman, signed up for a security job in Iraq at the British Embassy. It meant the first entry of Fulbrook's CV was: reporter on the *Baghdad Times*.

In 1961, he got a job on the *Worcester Evening News*, as a sport sub-editor, in the days the newspaper was in its romantic, turreted, offices in Trinity Street in the city centre.

For ten years Fulbrook was both Worcester City club secretary and football correspondent for the *Worcester Evening News* raising questions of a conflict of interest, but only from outside the club. He was City through and through; he even reported on an away game on his wedding day in 1967. The *Malvern Gazette* reported in his obituary in 2013, how he got married at 9am at Worcester Register Office and then jumped in his car to cover City's away game against Chelmsford City.

Fulbrook was a character, to say the least. He may have had his critics, but he was one of those people who work for football clubs, for very little money, largely because he loved the game.

My father knew him well and told me a story once how he was phoning in the Worcester City team, before a game against Stourbridge at Amblecote, to a copytaker sometime in the 1970s.

For the benefit of the digital generation a copytaker was a person sitting at the other end of the phone who would type out your dictated story on a piece of paper and hand it to the news desk to be edited for publication. Hard to believe, I know, but all journalists did it up until the 1990s.

The team sheets were also a world away from the slick digital graphics of today. Teams were scribbled on a piece of paper by the manager or the club secretary or anyone with a pen.

There was only one substitute in those days and often the manager didn't bother to scribble down the name of the No. 12.

This was my father's problem as he filed the team down the phone to the *Sporting Star*, a Saturday sporting pink paper. In his dilemma he looked right and saw his journalist friend walking into the ground.

'And substitute, number 12 ... P. Fulbrook,' he told the typewriter-rattling copytaker at the other end. You could get away with that kind of light-hearted stuff in those days when non-League football was not as serious as it is now.

'Some days later, I had a call from Peter saying he was treasuring a cutting from the *Sporting Star* but was disappointed I made no mention of him during the match!' chuckled my father a lifetime later.

Most City fans were very happy with enthusiastic Fulbrook's reportage that splashed across the back page of the *Worcester*

Evening News every night; words which did offer in-depth coverage of the, mostly, glorified City success and minimised their shortcomings.

Other clubs were green with envy. I recall the expansive Kidderminster Harriers director Colin Youngjohns berating the fastidious journalistic impartiality in my reports for the *Kidderminster Shuttle* from Aggborough. A storyline he never tired of.

'What we need is someone like Fulbrook. I once saw him write a report about City losing 5-0 claiming City were firing on all cylinders when the opposition had five lucky breakaways!' Youngjohns used to say in the Harriers social club after a couple of pints.

When it came to bogus attendance numbers, Fulbrook was the prince of underestimation.

I remember former Worcester City coach, the late Graham Newton, telling me during his Stourbridge days in the 1980s: 'The crowd would be hanging out of the pylons at St George's Lane, and I'd ask Peter how many? He used to look around and say 800. Unbelievable!'

Even Barton questions the 8,253 official attendance for the game of his life against Plymouth Argyle in the cup.

'I'll be able to come up with the official attendance next time we speak, Chris, because I've only got a few more to count,' says Barton with his tongue firmly in his cheek.

On the pitch, a few quid here and there didn't matter against Plymouth; semi-professional pride was at stake.

'It was just one of those days where everything went right for us and everybody played to their potential. Yeah, it was an unbelievable day. I always remember walking out and there – it was full to the pylons – and wondering, "Gosh where did all these people come from?"' he says.

'You think, gosh, the pitch was the size of a postage stamp; or, at least, it felt like it!'

Worcester City oozed confidence as they took to the game with a will, amid deafening roars from the crowd.

In the 13th minute, Malcolm Phelps, a £100 signing from Nuneaton, leapt like a young salmon to head home a corner to make it 1-0. One of the most important of the 93 goals he scored in the eight years he spent at City; he played in every position, including a full game, at Scarborough, in goal.

Bearded, swift and tricky Jimmy Williams sealed the game. For the entire match Worcester City's star striker had confused and unsettled the Plymouth defence with his fast, jinking runs; he scored in the second half and the ground erupted. In those days of freedom and lax safety, people were carried for scores of yards as the crowds pushed forward in jubilation.

A 2-0 win and headlines in the national press.

As Bob Geldof, who was number one at the time, could have sung: 'It's a Rat Trap Malcolm! ... and you've been caught!'

As the final whistle blew, the reaction depended on where you stood. At the Canal End, furious Plymouth Argyle supporters dismantled the pitch barriers in protest. The rest of the crowd invaded the pitch in sheer joy.

'I don't think you could get off the pitch at the end, it was just a brilliant, brilliant, day; one to cherish,' says Barton with a smile 46 years later.

As the Worcester City changing room buzzed with victory the man in the fedora was to have the last word.

"It was a wonderful, wonderful day,' says Barton.

'I always remember after the game, in the dressing room. I remember Malcolm Allison, one of the biggest characters in the game; he was a big bloke, as well, and he came in the dressing room. He filled the door, and just stood there for a few seconds. Talk about someone who can hold an audience, and everybody shut up and just looked at him; and he just said "well done" turned round and walked out.'

Fair play, thought the City players. A few days after the game, the Football Association upheld Allison's fourth appeal and lifted the more than ten-year touchline ban. Fair play, FA.

Surprisingly, Allison survived humiliation in Worcester and didn't leave Plymouth until the new year when his old club Manchester City called him back for a third, ill-fated, stint.

For Worcester City, it was one of the most glorious nights in the club's history; the players were delirious when their manager Clark walked in with another pocket full of bone dust.

Clark gave the players £1,000 in cash to share ahead of a long night out.

'I was only a young kid, so they just put a rope around my waist and took me to the local pub not far from the ground,' says Barton.

When Worcester City drew Fourth Division Newport County away in the second round of the FA Cup on the following Monday, Clark told journalists he would give even more cash for another cup win.

Ironically the Plymouth game didn't get the wide coverage it deserved in the provincial press because the journalists were on strike. The late Paul Ricketts, who spent 48 years as a sports reporter on the *Worcester News*, volunteered to man one of the gates at St George's Lane, just so he could see the match, but couldn't write a word on the game.

The win over Plymouth was bittersweet for Barton. It was the last game he would play in the blue-and-white stripes of Worcester City, in which he had been so happy.

'That Sunday after the game, I got a phone call and Nobby Clark says, "Peter Fulbrook is picking you up tomorrow; we've agreed a deal!" I said: "Manchester City?" They had been watching my games and I just assumed it was Manchester City. I sat on the stairs, took the phone call and it was near the end of the phone call I said: "Oh blimey, we're going up the M6 to Manchester?" and Clark said, "You ain't going to Manchester, you're going to Everton!" 'Oh right, OK," says I,' recalls Barton.

Goodison Park was huge and a world away from Worcester City, pulling an average of more than 35,000 for every game in 1978/79.

Nearly half a century later, Barton admits he was overawed.

'Chris, I was shitting myself. Gordon Lee was the manager, and he took me up in his office. I said, "Oh my God, what the bloody hell am I doing here?" And the secretary comes in, "Would you like a cup of tea?" I said: "yes please!" and it was bone china cups and saucers and Gordon Lee went out; I'm having a sip of this tea and honestly I'm shaking like a jelly, and yeah, I got talking to him and not one of his agents, it was just me and him on our own. If he had said "I'll give you 20 quid," I still would have said yes'and he said, "Oh, hey, no you haven't finished your tea!" I can't say, "Oh no, I don't want it," and I can't pick it up cause I'd be playing "God Save the Queen" by shaking out the tune on the cup,' he says.

The deal was done, and Barton drove back to Worcester with the cheque in his pocket. Imagine that in the modern game? In his heart he carried a good deal of humility.

'I look back at that team and there were Barry Williams and Kenny Lawrence. In my book, if someone is willing to pay £30,000 for John Barton, I'd pay £130,000 for them. I mean the value for those players of that era today? God knows what those players would go for today,' he says.

There is still some dispute over how much Barton was sold for.

The official records of Worcester City say £27,500; Barton reckons it was £30,000 and the cheque was for £33,000 to take into account VAT and other costs. All everyone knew was this was a record for a non-League player and a vindication of the talent-nurturing at Worcester City.

What is clear is that manager Clark and club secretary Fulbrook thought it wasn't enough. They asked Everton for more but were told to take it or leave it.

Everton argued that Barton, whom Worcester City signed on a free transfer from Stourbridge, had no top-flight experience, at the age of 25. Years later, Fulbrook told a colleague at Worcester City that Clark felt short-changed and angry as they stomped out of the Goodison Park offices.

On the way out, Clark spied a brand-new electric typewriter, unattended, on one of the desks.

'We're taking that with us!' he said. Fulbrook unplugged it, put it under his arm and put it in the car to take back to Worcester.

The deal was done, and Barton served his notice at the Birmingham company, where he worked as an engineer, and headed north.

'I always remember the first day I drove up to Liverpool in an old clapped-out Morris Marina and I got to the training ground and thought, "Shit, where do you go from here?" As I got to the door one of the coaches said: "Are you the lad from Worcester? Get changed,"' he says.

'I went in the dressing room and all I could see was internationals: Bob Latchford, Colin Todd, George Wood, Mike Pejic, Dave Jones, Dave Thomas and Andy King. A breath of fresh air.'

Barton wasn't alone; he spent his first day with two players from the side Worcester City humbled a few weeks before. Everton had signed Plymouth Argyle midfielder Gary Megson along with Martin Hodge, the goalkeeper who let two in at St George's Lane.

After three appearances Barton established himself in the swashbuckling right-back role and team-mate Todd predicted he would play for England.

'My first game was in the reserves against Bolton Wanderers at Burnden Park.

'I thought as they had spent £30,000 on me they were going to persevere with me. At the same time, they signed a lad called Gerry Mullan for £100,000 and they sent him back to Northern Ireland, so nobody was safe!'

The good news was the right-back slot was up for grabs. Everton had tried Terry Darracott, Colin Todd, Neil Robinson and Billy Wright at right-back; none had secured it.

Barton impressed in a sparkling appearance as substitute against Norwich City and started the last nine games of the 1978/79 season.

The players called him 'Special Agent'. For the younger readers among you, *Dick Barton Special Agent* was a 1940s radio serial, which was revived in the 1970s.

The next season, Barton was the man in possession. The penultimate game he played for Everton was against Dutch side Feyenoord in the UEFA Cup first round, first leg, in Rotterdam, on 3 October 1979, less than a year after Barton left Worcester City.

Everton lost 1-0. The official Everton report sheet from the game said of Barton: 'Worked hard and laid some good balls off. His finishing is not there, though.'

'From playing for Worcester City to playing against Feyenoord at Goodison in the European Cup, that is the stuff of dreams,' he says.

The shattering of this dream was swift and cruel. Just three days later, at Coventry City on 6 October 1979, Barton was carried off with the agony of a broken ankle.

The injury didn't heal properly. Barton wasn't fit again until 5 October the following year, by which time talented young right-backs Brian Borrows and Gary Stevens had taken his place. He played 69 games, with one goal, for Derby County, but wasn't the same again. Barton played fewer than 30 games for Everton, but says it was an honour.

'If I had the winning lottery ticket and you asked me to swap it for my memories, I would tell you to stick the ticket where the sun don't shine.'

Worcester City soldiered on, without star right-back Barton, to the Newport County game on 16 December 1978. That December was the wettest month in England and Wales since 1934 with temperatures dropping to minus 8 degrees; a cold and foggy month, according to the Met Office.

On the morning of that day, with Christmas lights shimmering in the shop window, my father dropped me off in Worcester early for the coach journey to Newport County. I wanted to call in at Warmans, in Mealcheapen Street, to buy a paper bag of Gray's Herbal Tablets. We believed, in those innocent days, that these sugary sweets would keep out the cold.

There I was, a fairly sensitive and impressionable youth aged 15, but looking younger: hair over my collar, flared jeans, a V-neck jumper and a blue hooded parka in the hope of staying warm.

It was a short walk to the main thoroughfare into the city from the north. In the Tything, right outside the old Alice Ottley School, there was a line of waiting buses, growling with idling engines spewing clouds of diesel into the winter air.

I sat near the front of one of the Newport County-bound coaches with my schoolfriend Nick Hill. We spent a lot of our spare time debating Southern League football in the playground and now we were going to an historic game. Also, his dad wouldn't let him go alone, so, he asked me to go with him; aah, different times.

Outside the window, the street was thick with striding, strutting City fans ready to board the buses.

This was the late 1970s. Many had long curly hair down their backs and Zapata moustaches, nearly all wore blue-and-white scarves; there were no replica shirts in those days. I would kill for a photograph of the fans on that day.

Change the clothes and you could have mistaken a few of them for a bunch of civil war cavaliers. At least, that's what my romantic head thought then.

'Makes yer proud,' said my mate Nick, with a nod, from my left.

It was like the gathering of an invading army. Most were smoking, a few were drinking; some stood in small groups on the pavement, bobbing their long hair, as they laughed through the pre-match gossip, with a fag between thumb and forefinger.

Nick's father was a Worcester man who had supported City since the war. In his married life he had transformed into a gritty farmer scratching a living from sheep and chickens on land near Lineholt, a hamlet off the A449 between Worcester and Kidderminster a couple of miles from my family home in Hartlebury.

Like a lot of the Worcestershire men we grew up with, he was tough, but deep down a kindly soul of few words. He used to sit in the Brookside stand at St George's Lane, also like most adults then, with fag in hand.

'Roberts, yer bone-idle bugger!' he would stand up and shout, occasionally, at City's mercurial winger Dave Roberts, before sitting down and not saying another word all game.

On this day of the second round of the FA Cup he couldn't make the away game with Nick and I on the bus to Newport. This journey felt a bit like a rite of passage to manhood.

The bus ground out of the city streets and onto the A449 over the Malvern Hills with its stunning views over the county. More than once we drove past a parked bus on the hills with City fans lined up peeing out excess beer ahead of the two-hour journey. Of course, we all cheered and laughed.

It was a pleasant journey down through the thick forests near Ross-on-Wye and the wide green fields around Monmouth.

Heading into Newport was a stark contrast. It looked more like Eastern Europe than South Wales. Like a fairy tale, it was grim.

Someone once wrote that when you were going to a town for an away game you could tell how hard fans were by the grimness of the architecture; on this afternoon, you would expect the fans of Newport County to be made of granite.

It was overcast and dark as we pulled up outside Somerton Park. Stewards ushered us through the turnstiles, like the damned into Hades, into the poorly lit and fenced-in away terrace, in a corner behind the goal.

Somerton Park was reputed to be one of the most ramshackle grounds in Britain with a smell from the toilets you could never forget. It was.

The newspapers had built up this game. One report claimed there was going to be an all-ticket crowd of 14,000 at Somerton Park with a special train for 600 of an expected 6,000 away supporters. The official crowd was 7,196.

I stood on the away terrace on that day. I would say it was more like 2,000, with a roar of 10,000.

'City! City!' we shouted as the players came out to warm up.

'Jimmy! Jimmy! Jimmy!' came the chant at the first sight of Williams jogging along the touchline.

On the other side of the fence, a number of Newport fans spent most of the game on each other's shoulders spewing vitriol against the English.

The Worcester fans hit back calling the home fans – it sounds a bit quaint now – Taffs. This was a name for Welsh soldiers, bestowed without any slur, in World War Two, which references the River Taff that runs through South Wales.

'Oh, I'd rather be a Muppet, rather be a Muppet, rather be a Muppet than a Taff!' sang the City supporters to laughter from our side of the fence and silence from the Welsh side. It was all in good humour, especially in comparison to some of the spiteful and twisted chants of the 21st century.

It was a fairly unremarkable game of few chances with Worcester City shading it in the singing stakes.

'We'll see you down the Lane! We'll see you down the Lane!' sang the thousands of travelling supporters, as the final minutes ticked away, nodding their heads to each other with confidence and broad smiles. It was a sweet moment. Rarely have I heard a chant of such joy and pride in half a century of non-League football.

We nearly didn't see Newport County down the Lane. The last kick of the game at Somerton Park fell to Worcester City midfield general Barry Williams. He smashed a long-range shot against the bar that bounced clear; so close.

As soon as the final whistle blew, all headed from the ground in haste.

The reason? All the FA Cup games were played on the same day and the draw for the important third round that brought in the top-flight clubs would be broadcast live on national radio at 5pm.

Hundreds of us clambered into the coaches, parked side by side on the gravel, in the dark outside Somerton Park.

'Shhhh … shhhh…Sit down! Shut up!' came the cries from the front as we all craned to hear the clack of balls and growl of the man from the Football Association. It seemed to take an age for our ball to be pulled from the bag.

'Worcester City or Newport Country … will play … ,' you could cut the atmosphere with a knife.

'West Ham.'

All of the coaches erupted in cheers. It was as big as if the last-minute Williams shot had crept under the bar. People were standing up, shaking hands, from every seat on the coach next to us there seemed to be people with thumbs up and huge grins across their faces.

'West Ham! West Ham!' everyone seemed to be shouting, almost in disbelief. Trevor Brooking, Billy Bonds, Alan Curbishley and Alan Devonshire at St George's Lane? Players we had seen only on *Match of the Day* on Saturday nights; surely not.

Back in Worcester that night we talked about the prospects as we called in at Antonio's in Shaw Street, where we bought perhaps the best fish and chips I have ever tasted.

All Worcester City had to do was beat the lacklustre Newport County two days later at St George's Lane on 18 December. Monday night couldn't come soon enough for us.

This time, Nick's dad drove us there. Being a good farmer, he always liked to be early; therefore, we were in the ground sitting in our seats in the Brookside stand by 6pm.

In hindsight, it was a wonderful experience to see the ground fill up with the biggest crowd in nearly 20 years: 10,223 for a replay between a non-League club and a Fourth Division side which poured thousands of pounds into the grassroot game.

In 2024, Barton can't believe the FA scrapped replays.

'I was aghast, to even suggest it! I just thought, 'no!'. Foreign owners, they don't get the FA Cup, do they?. No, it's just stupid, and for what? For the sake of one game in some cases. That was the beauty of it, the romance the excitement, and you think, "We've got another chance" and now-no replays,' he says.

It was a bitterly cold night for the Newport County replay. Fog hung like a freezing blanket, and it appeared to be getting thicker. On top of that, there was that pall of cigarette smoke rising from the ground. In this health-conscious age, you forget that in the 1970s and 1980s, nearly all adults smoked, especially at football matches. From Wembley to Wealdstone, you would see a constant stream of smoke escaping from the stands into the night air.

A number of Newport fans were late getting into the ground and police walked a group of about 40 around the pitch to their spot at the Canal End. The City fans gave them a hostile reception and in defiance they held up a huge Welsh flag to boos from the Brookside.

From the kick-off, Worcester City were all over them. Midfielders Lionel Martin and Gary Stevens, who never seemed to stop running, built up attack after attack; it was a cultured approach on a night when the agricultural approach may have been better.

The fog thickened and waned all night, leading to questions over whether the game would be called off. One minute, you could see the main stand through the fog; the next minute you could hardly see the centre circle. Newport County tried to get back into the game and hit the woodwork with the Worcester defence at sixes and sevens.

The speed of Jimmy Williams again proved a headache for the visitors. They ran out of ideas to stop him. A crude tackle scythed him down, that would have been a red card these days. The offender didn't even get a talking to.

The free kick led to a goal that raised the roof. Barry Williams floated over a high ball and the unmarked Malcolm Phelps dashed in to head past the keeper. The ground erupted; the City players leapt on each other's shoulders in the fog. In the Shed stand, next to the Brookside, there was a massive push down the steps that left supporters tumbling and struggling to find their feet, including one of my best mates, now a retired teacher. He reckons the late Eddie Chadwick was behind it.

In the second half, City kept Newport at bay with ease. The time ticked past the 85th minute. All of a sudden, I was aware of the middle-aged men in the stand checking their watches, smiling and nodding to their children, or grandchildren, sat next to them. As each minute crawled by, the smiles were getting wider and the nods deeper. Worcester were coasting towards a home tie with West Ham and another 10,000 crowd in the third round.

Then came the 89th minute and disaster.

Phelps, the goalscorer, was on the ball, on the left-hand side of his goal near the brick wall at the Canal End. Everyone held their breath, as even though he was under no pressure, there were seconds to go.

In 2024, the striker would have just stood there and shielded the ball or go for the corner flag; usual time-wasting stuff (yawn).

Phelps didn't. Instead, he launched the ball dangerously near his own goal, I think, in an attempt to clear it. Fatal. Somehow it hit someone's head or body – I was there and I still don't know – and rolled, ever so slowly, into the Worcester City net. Someone, somewhere behind me said, 'No.'

The Official History of Worcester City FC has it down as an own goal. The next day, the *Birmingham Post* reported that the ball hit the head of visiting striker Howard Goddard.

The couple of hundred Newport County supporters behind the goal were in ecstasy. The Worcester City players looked like they'd been hit by a truck.

I can still see Stevens banging the palm of his hand down hard on top of his curly hair. The rest of the players walked around looking lost; they barely had time to kick off before the final whistle went.

Extra time as the temperature dived. The crowd around me roared City on but the Newport County players performed like men released from the gallows. Full-time professional fitness told and Goddard scored the winner with a towering header past Jim Cumbes at the Canal End; no doubt this time.

Four hours after taking my seat in the Brookside all 10,000 filed out of the ground more funereal than furious. The only home fans happy on the night were those who left early to avoid the traffic and went to bed thinking City had won 1-0 before getting a rude awakening from the newspapers the next morning. Ah, life without internet.

There was a bit of fighting spirit on the way out as a couple of Newport County fans in the main stand laughed and shouted: 'West Ham!' from a safe distance.

The bloke right next to me pointed his finger like a weapon dipped in contempt.

'You'll never beat them on that cowfield of yours!'

Well, Newport County did beat West Ham on their cowfield before more than 14,000 in January. West Ham stars Trevor Brooking, Frank Lampard senior and Billy Bonds went down like a sack of spuds, 2-1 at Somerton Park.

Newport's next opponent, in the fourth round, was Colchester United, a team destined to be relegated that season back to the Fourth Division. Now this is where my Worcester City v Manchester United theory comes in.

For some reason only the football gods know, Newport County drew the first game 0-0 at Somerton Park, in front of 10,000, before losing the replay 1-0 at Colchester.

This set up Colchester v Manchester United at Layer Road. Colchester had ample chances to take the lead against an honest, star-studded, United team, long before the foul idea of giving the kids a run because it's only the cup.

In the red shirt that night were internationals Gordon McQueen, Micky Thomas, Lou Macari, Martin Buchan, Jimmy Greenhoff, Sammy McIlroy – the last of the Busby Babes – and goalkeeper Gary Bailey.

On the night, United appeared vulnerable and scraped a 1-0 win thanks to a Greenhoff goal five minutes from the end.

Now, my sliding doors theory is this. If Worcester City had held on for 35 seconds longer to beat Newport County, as they should have done, I think City would have also shocked an out-of-sorts West Ham at St George's Lane.

As for Colchester in the fourth round, I think the 1979 Worcester City team – maybe the best ever – would have had them for breakfast.

Which would have left Worcester City v Manchester United at St George's Lane. What price an upset that could have gone down in history?

Unfortunately, life is not like that. We can dream.

Besides, you could argue Worcester City lived the dream of kicking legends out of the FA Cup 20 years before.

Chapter 22

How Worcester City Buried Liverpool

TAKE NOTE, this is going to be a pub quiz question one day.

Which is the only team in England to have a 100 per cent success record against Liverpool?

Answer: Worcester City!

Forget about Wembley; the Worcestershire club may not have played professional football, but the club ground the multiple European and English champions into the mud on an icy afternoon at St George's Lane in January 1959. The only non-League team ever to topple the Reds in the most embarrassing defeat in the Merseyside club's history.

The FA Cup clash against Liverpool was set up by a handsome 5-2 win over Fourth Division Millwall at home in the second round.

Mike Davis, a Worcester City fan since 1946, was at the Millwall game with his dad.

'What is possibly forgotten sometimes is that fantastic win against Millwall where for the first time, and probably the last, I saw my dad cry, simply because he was so excited,' he recalls.

It is hard to imagine in the 21st century such big sporting events captivating an entire city in provincial England. No one was trying to stream on illegal sites, no one was looking at their phones for alerts; no one could watch it in the pub, nor go to the garden centre instead, because there weren't any.

Instead, more than 15,000 people, about one in five of Worcester's population at the time, crammed into St George's Lane. It certainly brightened up the drab post-war world of make do and mend, where rationing had ended a mere five years before.

People queued for hours before the game; the streets around St George's Lane were jammed solid with hooting cars, bells on bicycles and people loud, happy, and on holiday from life. There were tickets to be had as many Liverpool fans, who couldn't leave work for the rearranged game on the Thursday afternoon, had returned theirs.

Schools, shops and factories closed for the day. Schoolchildren who had tickets for the game showed them to the headmaster to earn the afternoon off.

One of the factories closed was Froude, an engineering company near Shrub Hill Station.

Among the young engineers working for Froude on that day, was a young man by the name of Gerald Boddy, then aged 28.

The engineers could hardly believe their luck, when hours before the game they downed tools to cycle to St George's Lane with the blessing of their bosses.

'They told us we could go to the game as long as we came back to work afterwards to make up our hours,' recalls Boddy.

That was a bit harsh, says I, imagining the ruckus and resentment a similar request may cause today.

'No. We thought it was really generous. Besides, we needed the money!'

A different world.

Boddy, born in Cheltenham and bred in Worcester, worked as an engineer at Froude for 46 years, but sport is his passion.

I have known him for more than 40 years and he was a fine wicketkeeper, goalkeeper and umpire in his day. He was also a shrewd judge of a football match, who keeps active.

Twice a week, the 94-year-old strides from his home in St John's, across Worcester Bridge over the Severn, to the Crown in Broad Street for lunch with his friends.

This is where I caught up with him for a chat about the famous Worcester City cup run of 1959.

It was a game which burnished the resilience of hard-working men as well as part-time footballers. There was no pre-match conditioning for the Worcester City players.

Eight of the Worcester City team were working hours before the game.

Forward Eddie Follan, a Scot who played 36 games for Aston Villa, was a van driver. He fed his baby daughter before heading off to work at 6.30am on the morning of the biggest game of his life.

The game had been called off on the previous Saturday as temperatures plummeted. A layer of ice on the St George's Lane pitch threatened yet another postponement. It made the grassless pitch bone hard and ball control difficult.

It is fair to say that the conditions probably hampered the stars of Liverpool more than the Southern League players of Worcester City.

'Then the club had the wonderful idea of spreading salt on the pitch to thaw it out, which it did, but it became a sea of mud,' says Davies.

Also on his way to the game on that muddy, frosty afternoon was serving soldier Alec Mackie, who was a regular in the Worcestershire Regiment at Norton Barracks, just outside the city. He volunteered for a three-year stretch just after his 18th birthday, and became the fourth member of his family to serve in the regiment.

Mackie made a name for himself in Worcester with a long career as a journalist and local government official. As a soldier, he served in Kingston, Jamaica, with the first battalion of the Worcestershire Regiment, in 1957, followed by a stint quelling unrest in the Bahamas.

By January 1959, Mackie was back serving in Worcestershire.

'On the day before the midweek match, Norton Barracks was contacted by the club to offer ten, I think, free admission tickets for the standing enclosure to be allocated, by draw, to the 30 or so permanent staff serving at the depot,' he recalls.

'The draw was subsequently organised by the Depot RSM, Albert Foden. The raffle tickets were drawn from his cap, and I was one of the lucky ones. On the day of the match, the ten lucky soldiers, wearing their battle-dress uniforms and blue beret with the Regimental Badge over the left eyebrow, as per regulations, got into an army "three-tonner" truck and off we went to St George's Lane.'

Another fan on his way to the game was Tim O'Grady, later to be the club's photographer, who thumbed a lift from Kidderminster.

'I was working on the railway at the time,' he said 'and we managed to get a lift with a lorry driver who came from Liverpool.

'He parked in the city centre and then came to the game with us.'

Apparently, Liverpool weren't too chuffed about the days they spent in cold Worcestershire waiting around for a hiding to nothing, which they clearly didn't fancy.

Theirs was no modern-day half-hearted, second string, give-the-kids-a chance team put out for an FA Cup tie against a small team. This was a Liverpool team studded with internationals. It was also a team on a good run and pressing for promotion to the First Division.

Goalkeeper Tommy Younger was an international who played for Scotland just over a year later in the 1958 World Cup in Sweden. Striker Alan A'Court, an English international, also played in Sweden.

Jimmy Melia, who became famous as the flamboyant manager of Brighton, may have played only two games for England, but he scored 76 goals, from midfield, in 269 games for Liverpool and won the League into the bargain.

Like Melia, defender John Molyneux was also a big part of this promotion and championship in 249 games for the club.

Ronnie Moran, who played 343 times for Liverpool on the way to becoming part of the club's famous 'boot room' management team, was also in the side.

A Liverpool legend in the making was the chief coach. Bob Paisley spent a lifetime at Liverpool as a player, coach and eventually manager, in a career interrupted only by World War Two.

Paisley fought in the Royal Artillery in the North African desert and rode into Rome on the back of a tank, as part of its liberation, in 1944. He didn't return until 1977, when he led Liverpool to win the European Cup in Rome and mentioned 1944 in his pre-match talk.

All were out on the pitch at 3pm on that frosty day with a record 15,000 in the ground, although the real attendance was very likely thousands more.

The engineer Boddy was high up on the timber sleeper terracing at the side of the ground, overlooking the Brookside.

'I had my arms pinned down by my sides. There was such a crush, we could hardly move,' he says nearly 70 years later.

Most people remember tremendous surges by the crowd every time the ball went near the Liverpool goal. It would have been a safety officer's nightmare.

Mackie the soldier and his comrades were in the thick of it.

'We stood together behind the goal at the Canal End. My uncle, Bernard Lane, chairman or club treasurer, I can't remember which, watched from the comfort of the directors' box!'

One of those sweet ironies that keeps us all interested in non-League football came like a bolt from the blue.

With all the experience on show, it was the youngest player on the pitch who drew first blood.

Tommy Skuse had just turned 18. He was a left-winger and former trialist at Exeter City. Skuse was destined to score 41 goals in 139 games for Worcester City before moving on to Bath City.

'He was a little dasher, not a bad player at all,' recalls Boddy.

Skuse was seen as the baby of the Worcester City team and wasn't one of the most popular players at St George's Lane.

'There was a group of supporters by one of the corner flags. They used to barrack Tommy Skuse something terrible,' says Boddy.

Yet, it was Skuse who raised the roof on St George's Lane after just ten minutes, by taking advantage of what the newspapers called 'a comedy of errors'.

City's Eddie Wilcox hit a long, low pass into the Liverpool penalty area. Defender Molyneux misdirected a pass back to Younger. There was a misunderstanding and when Younger realised, he made a lunge for the ball and lost his footing. This allowed Skuse to nip in between floundering goalkeeper and wobbly defender to smash the ball into an empty net at the Canal End. You could hear the roar in Gloucester.

In the next 20 minutes, Liverpool settled down and asserted their authority.

Yet a number of outstanding individual performances kept Worcester City in front.

Home goalkeeper John Kirkwood made a string of outstanding saves. The former Reading player was reckoned to be one of the best and bravest keepers outside the Football League, in the days when referees gave them scant protection. In 1957, it was still legal to barge the goalkeeper into the net, ball and all, if he didn't have both hands controlling the ball. A goalkeeper could be raked by studs, shoved over and punched without the referee speaking to anyone.

Kirkwood, a plasterer by trade, came up hard school as a keeper for a miners' team back home in Falkirk.

'Johnny Kirkwood was a great keeper who had elbows and knew how to look after himself,' says Boddy.

Les Melville, at centre-half, kept a lock on Liverpool striker Louis Bimpson. The newspapers called Melville 'a rock' on an afternoon when friendships counted for little.

'I was brought up in Liverpool and played for Everton. Centre-forward Louis Bimpson is my best pal, but not out there!' Melville told the *Daily Mail* in an issue dated 16 May 1959.

Friendship worked the other way in the crucial Scottish link-up between City's van-driving Eddie Follan and Sammy Bryceland. The two passed and moved like a dream to keep possession and the Liverpool players at bay.

'No wonder,' Bryceland told the *Daily Mail* after the match. 'We played together for Greenock boys' team and went 150 games without defeat!'

Another decisive factor was Eddie Wilcox at right-back, a Welshman who signed from West Bromwich Albion and took no prisoners. He had arrived at Worcester City during the club's ambitious spending spree in 1951 and stayed on to graft his way to becoming a club legend.

'Alan A'Court, a former international, was marked out of the game by City right-back Eddie Wilcox. A'Court wouldn't go near him on that day,' recalls Boddy with a laugh.

The City victory was not only down to heart, it was also down to canny preparation.

Worcester City captain and Wales international Roy Paul, who had lifted the FA Cup with Manchester City less than three years before, had watched Liverpool three times in the run up to the game. His plan was for his players to run at Liverpool and unsettle them. At the heart of this plan was City's man-mountain goalscorer Harry Knowles. The fans used to call him 'Knowles for goals,' and he fired in 148 in 200 games for City. He had speed and mobility that made him a battering ram of a centre-forward, in the vein of former Aston Villa striker Peter Withe.

'Harry Knowles, all knees and elbows; he could rattle people, very quick. He went to Cardiff, and they tried to teach him to play football, holding the ball up and such, but he stopped scoring goals!' says Boddy.

On this big occasion Knowles may not have scored but he helped deal the killer blow as the cold intensified in the second half and the minutes ticked away.

With eight minutes to go, Bernard Gosling, a former Portsmouth inside-forward, swept the ball over to Knowles. By rights, the Liverpool defence should have cut it out.

Knowles didn't need asking twice. He cut inside and whipped the ball into the Liverpool penalty area.

Liverpool defender White tried to cut out the cross from Knowles, but only managed to lift the ball over the head of Younger in goal. Younger twisted in the air to try to keep the ball out but landed in the back of his own net a split second after the ball. 2-0. The crowd went wild and the prospect of another big club, Sheffield United, at home loomed large. In the euphoria, on this cold day, anything seemed possible.

Two minutes later, Liverpool scored and were back in it. Centre-half Melville, a tower of strength throughout the game, charged into Liverpool's Freddie Morris in the penalty area. Melville claimed afterwards he was merely trying to protect his own keeper from an onrushing Liverpool player.

Geoff Twentyman put the penalty away to usher in the longest six minutes in the history of Worcester City. Tension was high on the terraces; some fans couldn't watch as the home team clung to their lead.

The referee blew his whistle for a free kick and thousands leapt over the barriers thinking the game was over. It took police and officials a couple of minutes to clear the pitch.

When the referee put the whistle to his lips for the final time there was no stopping the crowd. An estimated 10,000 people swarmed on to the pitch and carried captain Roy Paul and his players off shoulder high.

'I think the outstanding player was Roy Paul and the way he led the team. But they were all great players, great professionals,' says Davis.

The emotion was intense at the end of a game making international headlines. Many people wept amid the cheers, including Davis's sister and a group of other young fans.

'On his way off the pitch, captain Paul put his arm around them and asked whatever was the matter,' recalls Davis.

'I suppose I shouldn't swear, but what Paul actually said was, "We beat the fuckers – what's the matter?"'

It took nearly an hour for the huge crowd to filter away past the terraced houses in the narrow streets leading from the ground.

'After the match, we struggled through the crowd to meet up with our driver and jumped in the back of the truck for the return trip to barracks. I think some of the lads remained in the city to join the celebrations in the local pubs and returned to barracks after the pubs closed at 10.30pm,' says Mackie of the Worcestershire Regiment.

Inside the dressing room a St George's Lane, the Worcester City players passed around a bottle of champagne.

As they did so, Howard Yates of the *Liverpool Daily Post* dictated these words down the telephone line to his newspaper: 'When all the allowances have been made for, the hard ground and the near misses that could have been turned into goals, the fact remains that Worcester were the better side and were full value for this shock triumph.'

A few minutes later the Liverpool goalkeeper Younger went into the Worcester City dressing room to shake hands and say the better team won. Sportsmanship at its finest.

At about the same time, engineer Boddy was pedalling with his workmates back to Froude at Shrub Hill.

'Back to work we went, for two hours, and we were happy. We couldn't afford to lose two hours' work to start with and we thought the firm was being quite generous,' he says.

Not so generous to his own players was the Liverpool manager Phil Taylor. He said after the game: 'We lost because our forwards had no fight. We have no grumbles about the ground, which was as good as any in the country of this time.'

The following November, Taylor stepped down from the job for health reasons.

A few weeks later, Liverpool appointed Bill Shankly as manager and the rest, as they say, is history.

It is not too much of a stretch to suggest that the defeat at Worcester City ushered in a need for change which culminated in Shankly fashioning Liverpool into a modern top-flight club which dominated English and European football for a quarter of a century.

The prize for Worcester City was Sheffield United and another big day with another record crowd.

For the Sheffield United game, nine days later, 17,042 squeezed into St George's Lane (anecdotal evidence says it may have been as many as 20,000). Again, there was very little regard for safety as most clubs across the country packed them in while they had the chance.

Sheffield United based themselves in the Raven Hotel in Droitwich, Worcestershire. for a week before the game, which would never happen in this century.

Sadly for City, the fairy tale turned sour. It was to be the fourth round of the FA Cup and no further.

'Sheffield were a good side. Harry Knowles never had a kick. Their centre-half and left-back; very good footballers. Then there was their goalkeeper who played for England: Alan Hodgkinson. Up front they had Derek Pace. They called him "doc" because when he did his national service, he was in the Royal Army Medical Corps. He was quicksilver,' says Boddy, who was on the terraces again.

Sheffield United were too quicksilver for Worcester City on the soggy St George's Lane pitch.

It was 2-0 and the Sheffield manager Archie Clark said it could have been 5-0.

'To me, it was a racehorse against a donkey,' he said after the game.

The donkey simply said the better team won.

Chapter 23

Que Sera Sera – Worcester at Wembley

THE FIRST week of April 2024 brought forth floods and storms over Worcestershire, but Worcester City fans were calm. It had been a cracking week.

In the first few days of the month, City had beaten the weather, broken a 95-year-old record, all but wrapped up the Hellenic League and taken a huge step towards the club's first ever appearance at Wembley.

Six points clear, with four games in hand. It was 6 April, the day of the first leg of the semi-final of the FA Vase at Sixways, the home of the defunct Worcester Warriors Premiership Rugby team. It is a modern, clean and well-built stadium; perfect for a big game like this. Besides, a week of downpours left Claines Lane sodden as usual.

Worcester City tuned up earlier in the week, at Sixways, with a 7-0 thrashing of ten-men Roman Glass St George, Bristol's oldest and smallest football club, founded in 1868.

Worcester City's goalkeeper Haydn Whitcombe – so steady between the sticks all season – barely had a shot to save.

'We could have had a few more,' said Worcester City's manager Chris Cornes, without a hint of irony.

There was history made on the night too. The third goal, a lovely flowing move down the right finished by the trusty left boot of Worcester-born Kyonn Evans, was the 170th of the season, breaking the previous club record set in the 1929/30 season.

Kyle Belmonte also helped himself to a hat-trick on the night, Liam Lockett struck again, and Dylan Hart made it seven with a penalty near the end.

Twenty-five-year-old Belmonte, who has a sublime touch on the ball, was having the season of his life. By the first week in April he had scored 38 goals, with 17 assists, in 45 games.

OK, so the opposition wasn't that hot in a few of the games – as I saw with my own eyes – but, by my reckoning Belmonte has scored more goals in nine months for Worcester City than some score in a career. By this time, Lockett had scored 37 goals, with 21 assists, from the left wing! A tally any centre-forward would give his right arm for.

Just two days before, on Easter Monday, City beat Wantage away 3-2 after being 2-1 down with a few minutes left thanks to a last-gasp Jude Bellingham-style overhead kick from former League Two professional Izak Reid.

It seemed City couldn't kick wrong, as my father used to say, as the season neared its climax.

What a time for Worcester City to take another big step towards Wembley.

The semi-final brought Great Wakering Rovers forth from Essex. The village of Great Wakering is home to more than 5,000 souls, just outside Southend. It was built on clay that fed a brickworks that closed down in 1991. It must be a strange place to live – big swathes of land around the village are closed off and used by the British Army as a firing range.

Around 200 came up on coaches from Great Wakering waving the green and white.

'Took us five hours,' said one of the supporters in between sips of beer at the back of the stand before the game.

'We would have brought more, but they wouldn't let us bring people up to buy tickets on the day. Bullshit!'

We talked football for a few minutes, as friendly as you like, and then I asked how many supporters Great Wakering Rovers get for home games? About 80 came the reply; my face must have spoken volumes.

'At least we've got a ground!' retorted the oldest supporter among the green and whites and we all laughed. Non-League fandom at its finest.

As he spoke, more than 3,000 people were streaming into Sixways. It was the biggest crowd in Worcester for a football match since 4,027 attended the tearful last ever match at St George's Lane, in April 2013, that saw defeat against Chester.

A season that started on a low key with 487 at Claines Lane, on 1 August, bringing in a few thousand pounds in gate money.

On this day, Worcester City should have been looking at takings of probably more than £50,000, if you take into account the food and oceans of beer that were consumed on the day.

People told me after the game that the catering was done by another company affiliated with the former rugby club.

'But don't forget though, we also have to pay the fees to hire Claines Lane even though we are not playing there today,' said one of my mates who was stewarding the game. So, it was probably more quits for the City coffers at the end of the day.

Even so, the masses willing City on to Wembley – many of whom hadn't watched a City game in 20 years – were worth their weight in gold. It was hard to believe that the club was virtually dead just ten months before.

A huge roar, followed by thunderous applause, greeted the men in blue and white as they emerged from the tunnel with their arms high, applauding the fans.

Playing over the tannoy (why don't they work in non-League football grounds?) you could just about hear a nod to history through the din.

The DJ played 'Time is Tight' by Booker T and the MGs, the classic track that heralded hundreds and hundreds of games at St George's Lane. Whenever I have heard that track, whereever I have been in the world, I have always thought of Worcester City and home.

I could see the old main stand at St George's Lane in my mind's eye, from the Brookside, as the first few bars of the song played. Sadly, most couldn't hear it.

The captain Adam Mace ran with one arm aloft towards the fans across the bright green artificial turf, ahead of his players, clapping as he ran. A grand gesture: all that was missing was a white horse. I shook my head.

'Better than Premier League players who kiss the badge every week and then piss off to Italy!' said my college mate Graham Banks sitting next to me, a Worcester boy born and bred who has been watching City since the 1970s and with me since the early 1980s. I smiled knowingly.

My face must have betrayed my feelings. To be fair, it was all a bit much for me. It smacked of a victory parade three games too early. It tempted cruel fate.

The roar at kick-off was deafening. It was as if Worcester City, under the uncertain smile of the spring sun, would blow away the outgunned, outnumbered, not so Great Wakering Rovers. Hubris under clear blue skies.

The form book said City were top of the league and unbeaten in 24 games, since October; Great Wakering Rovers languished 11th in the Essex Senior League.

The game opened with sound and fury. City created a few rapid chances and looked dominant; each attack turning up the volume.

'Que sera, sera, whatever will be, will be, we're going to Wembarlee,' sang the Worcester lads at the back of the stand. Yeah, right.

Yet, for the first time in the club's history, this song seemed a racing certainty. There was a note of bombast among the Worcester City fans.

What happened next was one of the many reasons I love football, especially non-League football. A game far from VAR, played by butchers, bakers and tarmac makers. People who work hard for a living, on and off the pitch.

Youthful Great Wakering Rovers weathered the early storm and struck back against thunder. Steadily, the men in green-and-white stripes held the line in the early exchanges and probed patiently against City's confidence. The home fans went quieter and quieter with every probing move from the away side.

The moment that could have turned this game on its head was one to behold.

It came just before half-time; Great Wakering Rovers were enjoying a good period and City went from frustrated to struggling.

The quick feet of the green-and-white midfielder Hafeez Elegushi intercepted a pass across the back. He dashed towards a fateful one-on-one with the City keeper Whitcombe.

The crowd held its breath.

'No,' said someone behind me.

Elegushi ran like the wind towards goal. Shame, he was keen, he had scored only once that season in 27 games, a 54th-minute strike at home in a 4-3 win over Buckhurst Hill, to the delight of 66 people. This was a big moment for him before the biggest crowd he had ever played in front of.

He should have dinked it over the keeper, but jinked instead. His attempt to round Whitcombe ran a couple of yards too wide. He went for the byline, on the right, to cross to his flat-footed team-mate stranded in the six-yard box, who could have made a much better effort to challenge for the ball. That was my view as a paying customer. As I always say, you can score a hat-trick in your mind from the stands every week; on the pitch it is harder.

The run to the byline gave Whitcombe time to recover, dive, and claim the ball thankfully.

If Elegushi had scored it would have undoubtedly turned the match on its head. You can be sure he was kicking himself, for five hours, all the way home to Essex that night. He certainly looked downcast as he left the pitch.

'You miss chances in football, you have just got to keep going. Hopefully the next time he scores it,' were the words from captain Caiden Imbert-Thomas on BBC Radio Essex that night.

As the game wore on, goalless, through the second half, you could feel the anxiety building among the City supporters.

The deadlock needed a touch of magic to break it. It arrived 13 minutes – unlucky for some – from the end.

Hard-working Elliot Hartley, last season's player of the year, came on in the 72nd minute to inject urgency and flair into the midfield. His moment came in the 77th minute.

There was a throw-in from the left, Worcester City's midfield worked the ball neatly over to the right flank and played in Hartley lurking just inside the right corner of the penalty area.

Time seemed to stand still. The crowd drew its breath. Hartley, unmarked, turned and swung his sweet left foot through the ball, curling it into the top corner of the net. I was standing right behind the shot, and it almost made a perfect curve; it was beautiful. Pandemonium broke out in the stands as Hartley ran over to the blue-and-white ranks of Worcester City fans as his team-mates mobbed him.

Final score: 1-0. Worcester City had seven days to wait for a five-hour trip to Essex by the sea, not too far from Southend, for the second leg.

No peace for the non-League player. Days later, Worcester City travelled on a Tuesday night to wrap up the Hellenic League after months of record-breaking wins.

Hundreds of Worcester City fans followed their team down to Thornbury United, population 14,000, at the other end of the Severn Valley, just north of Bristol.

Worcester City needed just one point to secure the Hellenic League title. Thornbury needed a defence like a brick wall to stop them.

Surely, City supporters feared for their slightly leggy team as they faced a third game inside a week.

Thornbury, on the other hand, were eating humble pie, third from the bottom of the league.

You've guessed it, it was to be no walkover for Worcester City. One of the joys of grassroots football is that the divide between big and small teams is very narrow and even the lowliest teams can fight like lions.

Worcester City huffed and puffed until the 36th minute. Former Stourbridge striker Chris Knight latched on to a loose ball in the penalty area and smashed it home, as if it was his last kick in football.

A couple of near misses in the second half for City, but 1-0 it stayed, and the fans came on to the pitch at the end for a good-natured, joyful jig.

For most of them it was the first Worcester City championship they had seen in their lifetime, and all were happy in the knowledge it wouldn't be their last.

The players had worked hard all season; many of them had played more than 50 games in a settled side, which was tough to break into.

It was the first league title for Worcester City for 45 years. The last time was the Southern League Premier title, then arguably one of the top non-League titles in the land, back in May 1979.

'Bright Eyes' by Art Garfunkel was number one in the charts, thankfully eclipsed by Blondie with 'Sunday Girl' later that month. In the same month the film *Quadrophenia*, which gave birth to a new generation of born-again mods in Worcestershire, premiered in London.

When Worcester City won the Southern League, back in 1979 after a thrilling title race, the players were as whole-hearted and hard-working as the City men of 2024, but arguably they had a more physical game to play.

In a gruelling season of muddy pitches and flying boots, in 1979, Malcolm Phelps made 68 appearances – that's almost a season and a half for most top-flight English players these days – tireless runner Gary Stevens, 67, and bearded Kenny Lawrence 65. Fans used to call Lawrence 'Jesus' and he did look a bit like him. Sadly, a bone-breaking tackle ended Lawrence's glittering career as a player and thankfully he had a secure job with Wimpey the builders.

But there was no comparison when it came to the crowds of 1979 and 2024 in different times. When City clinched the Southern League title in 1979, nearly 10,000 people paid to watch the crucial last two games against Kettering and Leamington at St George's Lane. The 7,386 who came through the turnstiles for the Kettering game was the highest league gate since 1966.

It was merely hundreds down in Thornbury in April 2024, but the fervour seemed to echo down the years for a title securing a new lease of life for a club, all but dead less than a year before.

When Worcester City FC TV interviewed star player Jamie Insall, born and bred in Worcestershire, he simply turned to the singing, merry crowd, in the background and held out his right arm: 'That is what it is all about.

'We are returning to the promised land and let's give this fan base a day they deserve at Wembley,' he said.

The next morning striker Kyle Belmonte and right-back Logan Stoddard were back on their tarmac truck, piled high with wheelbarrows. On top of it was a placard retrieved from the previous night's celebrations: 'Hellenic League Champions 2023-24.'

'Back to reality in Lotto work trousers,' Belmonte wrote on X to his 1,300 followers.

There was plenty of work to do on and off the pitch in the busy week ahead.

The next leg of the route to Wembley stretched along the long winding road to Great Wakering Rovers in Essex on 13 April, where the Worcester City fans and players would be outnumbered three to one and far from welcome.

The game on the Saturday got off to an unfortunate start for Worcester City, before a ball was kicked.

Their manager and talisman was banned from the touchline. The football authorities charged the respected Chris Cornes with misconduct for an incident at a previous game. He denied it, but refused to appeal the ban for fear it would lead to a longer spell away from the touchline. Who would want to risk losing a spot in the dugout at Wembley?

Cornes wasn't at the ground in Great Wakering, he was banned from the game. One of his colleagues kept him in touch by mobile phone with one of the biggest games in Worcester City's history.

Around 1,500 people squeezed into Burroughs Park. More than 300 of them had spent hours on trains and buses from Worcester and were prepared to scream the place down.

Forgive the superstition, but the 13th minute of the game on the 13th day of the month delivered a kick in the guts for weary Worcester City.

Jake Gordon fired in the first for the green and whites to level the aggregate score at 1-1. A City defender blocked a shot in the penalty area. The ball looped up and Gordon waited a split second for it to come down before volleying over the unsighted Whitcombe's head and into the net with a dipping shot. It was a clever opportunistic goal, which turned the match.

Dylan Hart took advantage of a similar looping ball to head Worcester City back in front on aggregate, on 34 minutes, to the relief of the travelling fans.

'Worcestershire tra la la la! Worcestershire tra la la la!' they sang to the *Banana Splits* TV theme, even though most were too young to have seen it.

Despite this, the ascendency was with the county of Essex. It appeared to be only a matter of time before Great Wakering Rovers woke up to the superb and unexpected chance of getting to Wembley for the first – and probably last – time in their history.

All the home team needed was a late goal. It fell to Max Gnandi, who scored with a superb shot on the turn through a crowd of legs, in the penalty area, seven minutes from time to take the tie to penalties with the score 2-2 on aggregate.

Worcester City's destiny loomed large when Great Wakering Rovers hit the bar with their fourth penalty. This made it 3-3 in the shoot-out as one of City's best marksmen stepped up to the spot.

All Worcester City's top scorer Kyle Belmonte needed to do was put the ball in the net from 12 yards to put his team in a strong position. His deadly right boot netted 38 goals in the season so far. Surely?

The ground held its breath as Belmonte ran up. He put the ball a couple of yards wide of the left-hand post.

You would have bet your house on Belmonte. Instead the home supporters went wild with gloating glee as the ball sped harmlessly wide.

It wasn't over yet. Great Wakering Rovers scored the next penalty, cool as you like, before City's Calvin Dinsley scored to take the game to sudden death, before Rovers netted their fifth penalty.

Chris Knight – a veteran non-League striker and the scorer of the goal that sealed the championship for Worcester City – had to score to keep Worcester City in it. He missed and knelt in despair like a man looking for absolution from a priest. Many of the City players fell to their knees, a few in tears. Cruel fate.

The home players swamped Luis Shamshoum, the home keeper, born in Southend but registered as a Palestine international, in an eruption of joy. By contrast, the City players sat in a quiet group in the centre circle.

'Couldn't be any prouder of my players, they're gutted and so am I,' said Cornes of the defeat he never saw.

'Thanks for the fans that travelled; gutted we couldn't do it for you, but it wasn't for want of trying.'

Like many on that day, I couldn't get a ticket and was stuck in Worcester glued to the radio commentary from Essex.

Maybe City were over-confident, or simply too tired – it didn't really matter on this sunny spring evening, it was all done and dusted. Depressing.

I felt down. Like tens of thousands across Worcestershire, I really wanted to see City run out at Wembley for the first time.

I walked to Fort Royal Park high above the city to clear my head. I always find it a good, tranquil, place for introspection and perspective.

There was also an historical parallel. During the Battle of Worcester, in 1651, the Essex Militia in Cromwell's army stormed the Fort Royal, slaughtered its defenders and turned its cannons on the city to help win the battle. This bloody assault on Fort Royal despatched more than 1,000 enemies in an hour and turned the battle for Oliver Cromwell.

The men from Essex ran from their county to Worcester, in just 12 days, in a fit of Puritan fervour, for fear they would miss the chance to crush the Royalist rebels. In 2024, it was the men from Worcester who sped to Essex to be handed a crushing, if bloodless, defeat.

Nearly 373 years later, I stood in the sunshine looking at that wonderful clear view towards the cathedral that the doomed defenders of Fort Royal would have seen in their last hours. The seagulls wheeling overhead seemed to scream their disapproval of bloody battles lost.

To put it all into perspective, the same night Iran launched missiles against Israel. The world stood on the brink of yet another conflict.

Chapter 24

I know what you've done, you bastards

ON THE same day Worcester City's Wembley dream died, rivals Kidderminster Harriers suffered relegation from the National League.

The pain felt by City fans on the away terrace at Great Wakering Rovers was shared by the Harriers fans on the home terrace in Kidderminster. Neither saw it coming.

Kidderminster Harriers paid a high price for failure. A big-money move to bring in former Premier League manager Phil Brown, as a last-minute saviour, proved too little, too late.

Peter Fryar took it hard. It was another down day in 70 years of watching Kidderminster Harriers, where he is a life member, former director, former company secretary and passionate supporter.

The love supreme began in 1954. He used to play football behind the stands on the railway side and climb over the fence to watch the match for free.

His father, Charlie Fryar, was a well-known newsagent in Kidderminster; a business which the young Fryar started out in, before making a name as a publican.

I have known Fryar for more than 40 years, since I was a fresh-faced reporter in my first job on the *Kidderminster Shuttle*. We were close, without knowing it.

Our fathers were born in the same street in Bewdley, Worcestershire. We were born in the same hospital in Stourport, and he went to school with my auntie Daphne in Kidderminster. Oh, he won't remember it, but we both went to an away game in the FA Trophy at Barrow, in a smoky coach, on a rainy night in 1982.

Most people in football circles smile when you say the name Peter Fryar. He is an expansive and vivid raconteur with a strong, rich voice; a larger-than-life character who speaks his mind. He was always a mine of information in the stands at Kidderminster Harriers with a spice of speculation every now and again.

We journalists used to say if you cut him, he would bleed red and white; if Kidderminster Harriers ever appointed a French-style patriarch, Fryar is your man. The kind of football servant you can build a club upon and never afraid to get his hands dirty, the salt of the non-League earth.

'The one thing we all used to do, clean the dressing room, scrub the bird shit off the seats in the stand, before the season began, sweep everything. We used to roll the pitch with my car and a concrete roller. The supporters would be painting the walls and fences and we would get any leftover paint the council had got, and everything was painted dark red or dark green, because those were the colours of the borough. It meant that everyone was involved. Now, I regret there is less involvement. But it is more professional.'

Along with his lifelong friend and fellow director Colin Youngjohns, Fryar has worked tirelessly for decades to nurture his beloved club through everything from bankruptcy to modernisation. The two used to bring their lawn sprinklers to water the pitch in the days before proper irrigation.

'I couldn't do what they now do. Some bloke came up to Colin and myself one day and said: "Oi, you run this club on the back of a fag packet." And we said: "Yeah, at least its Benson and Hedges, not Woodbines!"

'It was on the back of a fag packet. We did some unlawful things, but never for our benefit.'

These were the days when every child and football player knew cigarette brands from a very early age.

'I've never smoked, thankfully, but you would go on the coach to Dover, or wherever, with the team and there would be myself and one player not smoking! The smoke was so thick you could not see the other end of the coach. But I suppose it didn't matter because the other team's players were doing exactly the same!'

There can't be too many football directors in the world who have roller-skated for miles and pushed a pram dressed as a baby in a bid to save their club.

Fryar has. He recalls roller-skating to an away game at Bromsgrove Rovers in 1976 to raise money to stave off bankruptcy.

It was a painful journey, as he could find only child-sized skates in the Kidderminster shops. He had to tape them fast on to his feet and they pinched like hell; they had to cut them off on arrival at Bromsgrove, to end the agony.

Pushing a pram, dressed as a baby, 14 miles to Worcester City proved even more arduous and thirsty work.

Fryar recalls a fellow director stood outside the Halfway House pub on the A449 holding out a pint for him with a smile. 'Lovely. I downed it and carried on,' recalls Fryar.

Both stunts raised money to save Kidderminster Harriers from extinction. A threat that reared its head more than once.

One time, Fryar recalls legendary Kidderminster Harriers club secretary Ted Gamson emerging down the players' tunnel in the main stand, looking over his shoulder, as bailiffs rummaged through the club offices. In his arms was his typewriter.

'They're not having this, it is mine!' Gamson said, shooting another glance over his shoulder. Fryar couldn't help but smile.

Fryar reckons Kidderminster Harriers went bust at least twice in his time.

'Every time Colin phoned me, when I was on summer holiday, I always thought: "Oh, no we haven't gone bump again, have we?"'

Some of the lengths Fryar and his fellow directors went to help Kidderminster Harriers progress surely wouldn't pass muster in today's regulated non-League game.

'It was always the right thing, not always in the right way,' he says.

'I'm saying that was the spirit of Stourbridge and Bromsgrove and every non-League club in the country ... Nobody, personally, was getting money.'

Fryar says the club took money out of the turnstiles to pay players and tried not to pay them at all in the summer. He says in the heyday of Worcester City in the 1970s, club secretary Peter Fulbrook used to take cash out the fruit machine in the social club before away games so he could pay the coach driver in 50 pence pieces.

'They were that far behind with the payments,' chuckles Fryar.

Take the time when Kidderminster Harriers were trying to get into the newly formed Alliance Premier League – now the National League – and found out they didn't have enough turnstiles to make the grade.

The resourceful Fryar found out Bedford United had gone bust and the wreckers were tearing down the Eyrie ground to make way for an extension to a brewery. He drove down to Bedford, in his Transit van, in the hope of getting his hands on a couple of rusty turnstiles.

'These turnstiles were free, they were going, and they wanted them out the way anyway. I managed to get them in the back of my Transit and brought them back to Aggborough,' he says.

'The brick entrance on Hoo Road hadn't got turnstiles, just someone collecting money, so we put them in because we were being ground graded for promotion to the Alliance Premier League. There were certain things you had to have, and eight working turnstiles was it. These two didn't work, but they looked like turnstiles.'

On the day two assessors arrived from the Alliance Premier League to check Aggborough, Fryar stood shielding the new turnstiles from Bedford.

'They counted a doorway on the other side of the ground as well as the two phantom turnstiles from Bedford. It made it eight as long as we only stood there and didn't try any of them.'

The two assessors completed their work and headed for the door of the boardroom as Fryar and Youngjohns stood by in hope.

'Just as they were going out the door, one turned to Colin and I, who were on the verge of going "Yeeess!!" One turned and said: "I know what you've done, you bastards," and if you let me down at the end of the season. I shall bloody go mad and drown the club.'

It paid off. The two dummy turnstiles did the trick and Kidderminster Harriers made it into the Alliance Premier League, then the so-called fifth division, from which it became the top club in Worcestershire and never looked back.

In all of this progress, the club needed quick cash like a man lost in the desert needs a drink.

A promise of new funds came with the humble scratch card in the early 1980s. I think I bought a few in my time; scratch the card, reveal a prize; or usually, nothing.

'We took other people's tickets and got commission on them and sold them. But then we thought we ought to run our own. So Dick Monger [a fellow director] went to London and found a printer of lottery tickets – and there weren't that many of them – he brought back brown boxes full of printed tickets, that was a month's supply of lottery tickets. The first prize was £1,000. We didn't have £1,000 in the club!'

It needed a bit of hometown cunning, which could have been written into an Ealing comedy.

'He [Monger] says, "The printer I found says that box there; the winning ticket is in there. There were a couple of thousand tickets in there. So don't issue that box until you have got a thousand pounds in the bank!" That is what we did for about two or three months. My wife and others were going around newsagents and pubs putting boxes in with tickets. She would go in every week and get the money back and put it in the bank account so we could pay the prizes out.'

It may sound chaotic, but the board of Fryar's day shrewdly reinvested handsome proceeds from cup runs and player sales.

The 1990s was a purple patch for Kidderminster Harriers. In the FA Cup, the club beat Preston North End and Birmingham City and ran West Ham close, before 9,000 people, in the fifth round at Aggborough. One of the highlights of these games was Jon Purdie dumping right-back and future Everton and Manchester United boss David Moyes on his backside in the lead-up to the winning goal.

I was lucky to see all three games, and delayed a trip to cover the war in Angola so I could see the fifth round. I must admit I had to pinch myself when I watched the highlights on *Match of the Day* that night.

Against West Ham, Kidderminster Harriers came within a split ace of becoming the first ever non-League side in the FA Cup quarter-final.

Transfermarkt calculations reveal the imbalance of the scales. The website reckons the West Ham side with Alvin Martin, Clive Allen and Lee Chapman was worth more than €454m, while the Kidderminster Harriers side was worth €50,000.

This brave team of tractor salesmen, telephone engineers and students pushed up everyone, deep in the game in a bid to beat the Premier League side with 12 internationals.

They held on, stretching every sinew, missing chances by a whisker.

With a replay on the cards, a long, hopeful ball from the wing found the head of Chapman, who headed it over the advancing keeper.

The Harriers players, who had run themselves ragged all game, flopped to the floor in despair.

The silence on the terraces was a deafening. A few rows ahead of me a supporter raised the palm of his hand before giving the kind of analysis that makes me hate the detached and mindless amateur analysis of the game. Utter rot.

'I'm sorry, but you can't play three across the back against West Ham,' he said.

Maybe not. But what about the pain and passion behind the move? What about the taking of risks in a bid to make history? What about working blokes, worth €50,000, taking a poke at a team packed with internationals, which shouldn't really have been on the same pitch? Isn't that the spirit of the game?

I'm sorry.

The cup run helped transform Aggborough from a ramshackle stadium with a rundown main stand built in the 1930s, into a modern stadium fit for the English Football League, to which the club was promoted fleetingly in 2000.

'We were really lucky when we were on the board. We went to Wembley; we won the FA Trophy. You played Wolves and Coventry in the FA Cup. You sold Lee Hughes for what became for us £1m in the end with the sell-on from West Brom on to Coventry.

'We had a percentage of that. We sold Forsythe to Birmingham for £250,000.

'We were very lucky to play in cup games,' he says.

This money helped usher in the full-time, professional, Kidderminster Harriers of the 21st century, which is organised on and off the pitch. All of this means a more expensive game; it now costs more for one month's football than it did for an entire season in Fryar's day.

Speaking of money, Aggborough stadium is now cashless – to the chagrin of more than a few fans – and a world away from its humble roots in 1886 when it amalgamated an athletics and rugby club to become Kidderminster Harriers Football Club.

Tickets are more expensive; huge black-clad security guards, dressed like they are policing pubs at chucking-out time on a Saturday night, tower over you at the turnstiles telling you to use another entrance.

Fryar still takes a keen interest in his club and lauds the involvement of businessman Richard Lane, the son of the late former club director Graham 'Rocky' Lane, who was on the board in my day. The son, who saw his first game with his dad when he was two, took over the club in 2019 and appears to be making a fair go of running it.

'That's the beauty of Richard Lane. He sometimes does appreciate the importance of supporters knowing the holistic heart of the club. You would think they are only interested in players, but they are not, it says a lot about how the club runs.

'Since Richard has taken over, it appears to be so stable. I have got one friend who works for the League and he goes to different clubs checking that they are running in accordance with the league and their finances are correct and all that … Percentage of wages to income, the League is pretty much in full possession of finances. He says it is so professional now. I don't even get a parking space when I come up here! The club is running really stably and when you have been through what you have been through in past years, that is such a joy.

'You can only congratulate Richard in making the club into a stable entity,' says Fryar.

Also, there is a legion of young men and women studying at the club as well as playing football. Old-school Fryar is enthused by this. 'You couldn't have League football without non-League football because of what non-League provides to the League. You look at it now, almost every club in the National League has got an academy of girls and young men,' he says.

'They do education and football every day and they can either go up to MVQ3, with Kidderminster College, or go up to degrees with the University of Worcester. So, the club get quite a big income stream off both ... They get money per pupil, and they then share that with the football club who really run the sports side of their pupils. We have people at the ground on physiotherapy and our medics also getting experience. There is sports analysis, there is videoing, social media and they do all of that; they do groundsmen, sports nutrition. They can take degrees.'

Fryar agrees with me that non-League football can catch talent that would otherwise be lost to the English game.

'All of those pupils are not going to be professional footballers, but there is no reason why they can't be sports scientists, video analysts and nutritionists and play for part-time teams like Hereford, Guiseley or Blyth Spartans. There is no reason why they can't earn a couple of hundred pounds a week playing and also have a full-time job.

'The beauty of it is, even if they don't make it to full-time football, they are educated and have a profession to fall back on. We get latecomers to the Harriers; they've been with Wolves, Villa or West Brom all of their nine years up to 18 and they've been told, "You are not going to make it." It may only be they are not going to make it playing the style of football that the club plays. At 18, they are devastated; they assume after nine years they were going to make it. One or two would sulk for a couple of years, then when they did come in, we have the second bite. We had some very good players, but only because they have been thrown out by the professional clubs.'

Kidderminster Harriers is by far the premier non-League club in Worcestershire and is likely to stay top dog for many years to come. It is organised and forward looking.

'For me, and probably quite a few others, what I love about it is young kids aren't going to be dumped on to the scrapheap when they are told they can't become full-time footballers that they've had this dream of all the way through, from four years old. It is great that they are educated and train every day. They live almost like a full-time footballer.

'I think that's incredible that they've lived the life, got an education, they can get a part-time playing position and they've got a career.'

'But hasn't it lost something along the way?' I ask Fryar, a man who has lived and breathed the club for nearly 70 years.

'The downside really is you are not so close to the club. I think with a lot of non-League supporters, whether they have been on the board, like I have, or not, you are in the end just a fan. And I think that there's more distance between supporters and the club than there used to be. It is more like a League club,' he says.

'There are very few players from Kidderminster. In the current squad there are six young kids who have come through the academy. The higher up the leagues you go the less chance of this there is. How many Manchester players play for Manchester United – two? Manchester City? Less.'

A sobering thought. Every non-League club wants to get on. It is only natural. The price is not just money, it can also mean selling something of the club's soul.

Chapter 25

'There's lies, and politics':
Giving up the Professional Game
for Worcester City

THERE ARE probably scores of electricians in Worcestershire, but I fancy there is only one who can glide past a handful of footballers – as if they are statues – and smack the ball into the top corner from 25 yards.

I know, I have seen him do it; even a Jude Bellingham bicycle kick!

Step forward quicksilver winger and former professional footballer Izak Reid, a skilful part of Worcester City's renaissance championship season. You could always tell he was a cut above the league he was playing in; he has pace and a sweet first touch.

I meet Reid on a warm summer afternoon in the leafy village of Ombersley, about six miles north of Worcester, deep in the Worcestershire countryside. We chat over a coffee at Checketts in the centre of the village, a café that used to be one of the best butcheries in the county.

My late grandmother always got her Christmas turkeys and beef from there and would tell us proudly several times over the festive table: 'This is Checketts!'

The assistant in the shop tells me that the butchery closed down months before after more than a century of trade. The shop famous for chops and steaks now serves cappuccino and sandwiches.

'Everyone buys their meat in the supermarket now,' says the assistant with a tinge of sadness and resignation. I can't disagree; progress, I suppose.

This end of an era was big news in Ombersley, where time may not stand still, but moves very slowly as the village hardly grows at all. When I was a kid, the adults used to say it was easier for a camel to pass through the eye of a needle than it was for a planning application for houses in Ombersley to pass through the council.

Is this village that time forgot a place for a young, fashionable, footballer to live?

'Yeah, It's nice. I'm from Stafford, which is a small town, and that's kind of all I've known. So, I'm not one for the city. I do like to visit London, Birmingham, do shopping or whatever, but I also know, when all's said and done, there's a big part of me is always glad to drive away,' he says.

Here, in Ombersley, Reid is probably also one of the few non-League footballers in history to live in a massive stately home set in 39 acres. He lives with his partner, Amy, in the 300-year-old Grade I listed Ombersley Court, the former country seat of the influential Sandys family, who fought for the king in nearby Hartlebury and Worcester in the English Civil War. In his flight from his catastrophic defeat at the Battle of Worcester, 1651, King Charles II was said to have paused at the post black-and-white timbered Kings Arms in Ombersley, which serves beer to this day for a king's ransom, to take bread and a pint of beer in the saddle.

Ombersley Court also played host to the Duke of Wellington in the wake of his victory over Napoleon at Waterloo.

When Lord and Lady Sandys passed away, in 2017, the rundown stately home went on the market for £3.5 million; the price of a three-bedroomed terraced house in Chelsea, according to estate agents.

Amy's family bought it with plans to hold events never likely to go down well in what is called Britain's poshest village, home to fewer than 2,500 people. Ombersley doesn't have streetlights and the average home in this exclusive village will set you back around £680,000.

The *Daily Mail* reported in April 2023, that Ombersley villagers were worried about a planning application to stage events at the stately home that could run past midnight, a time when most villagers have been tucked up in bed, for a couple of hours, at least.

On this afternoon in Ombersley, Reid is relaxed in the afterglow of the first league title for Worcester City for 45 years in which he scored eight times from the wing in 44 games.

'Yeah, and the good thing we created, was like a fear factor, so especially, when clubs came to Claines Lane, they were already defeated, straight from the off,' he says.

'They were wasting time, and you can hear players talking amongst themselves, going like, "we're happy for a draw". For me, you play football to win regardless of the level of your team, against another opposition like, you play to score a goal, and that was hard to take, so at times that was difficult, teams just came and defended against us, so we'd always felt like we'd beaten them before they'd begun, and you could sense that.'

Reid is a very likeable character who has been around the block in the professional and semi-professional game; he retains that pragmatism and humility, which can be scarce in athletes who often run on ego.

On this evening he is seriously contemplating his footballing future. Promoted Worcester City will be playing a step higher in the Northern Premier League and he is uncertain whether his 36-year-old legs will be retained for the next season. On this mid-summer evening, there is a nip of professional uncertainty in the air. Manager Chris Cornes asked his players to send him a WhatsApp message on the group saying if they wanted to stay or leave the club to save time drawing up the retained list. Reid was one of the first to do so.

'Yeah, nothing yet. They said hopefully by the end of this week, Sunday, we should all know where we stand.'

His feelings?

'I don't know really. I suppose age is always a factor, but then I suppose, if you still want experience in a team, things like that, and know how, then ... I don't know so probably then, 50-50, I wouldn't be surprised if there's a no.'

On this day he sounds a little doubtful.

'I've played higher level, because of the quality of how you are, and who you are, so, I feel like ... that's never been an issue, then again, I suppose then for the gaffer, I suppose it's just a case of younger, fitter, players ... I suppose I'm fit, but um, you know what I mean...?'

Reid says he'd be happy to go out on a championship high and get on with building up his work as an electrician. He takes a level-headed view of his playing career, which has seen him running across football pitches for money for half his life; the best part of 18 years.

When he was a child growing up in Stafford, it was all he wanted. More than that, he wanted to play for Manchester United.

From the age of six, every night he was out on the green, near his home in Stafford, dressed in his Manchester United kit, with his elder brothers Levi and Ishmale.

They played until it was dark and then Izak would go to bed dreaming of playing alongside Andy Cole and David Beckham.

For Izak and his brothers, football was bred-in-the-bone. Their father, Stan, came to Wolverhampton from Jamaica with his parents when he was 11.

Stan Reid spent his working life as a security guard, but at weekends he ruled parks and recreation grounds as a combative forward.

'Yeah, I think he played semi-pro, a winger, a forward player, a bit of a Wayne Rooney, quick and direct. He'd always say, "You lot are not quick enough to lace my boots!" We were a product of our environment where my dad loved football and Man United, my dad loved sports, cricket, tennis, all this stuff, and we were a product of him, so, oh, my dad loves football, so I love football, and obviously, I enjoyed it.'

They called Stan 'The Bull' and in a different era he could have made football his living like his sons.

'From speaking to his close friends and stuff they were saying that my dad was brilliant. But back in the day, he never had the backing, cause my nan was very religious, she was very like, church and studies first before football. I think he had approaches from Villa, if I remember right, for trials and things like that, different clubs in the area, but he never had that backing from his mom, so it never came to fruition. But I know through Sunday league and playing around the leagues and stuff everyone speaks in admiration of how good my dad was,' says Izak.

'Every Sunday we'd watch my dad, and the minute half-time comes, me and my brothers, would run on to the pitch, take shots in the goals at each other, for 15 minutes, and then run back off the pitch and then, when the game would finish, we'd run back on, and do the same thing again, because we just lived and breathed football.'

Izak was inspired enough to join nearby Stafford Falcons, on the bottom rung of the game, to hone the discipline and skills which would carry him to professional footballer. He was driven by a desire to play the game and the success of his brothers, in making inroads into the professional game, spurred him on.

'My oldest brother Levi went on to play for Port Vale, Oxford, Macclesfield with me for a season. My other brother Ishmale: Port Vale, Rushden and Diamonds. So it was a case of like my dad loved football, then Levi played football, and Ishmale played football, well I'm going to play football, and then seeing those guys go on and get a YTS [Youth Training Scheme] as it used to be back in the day, as a scholarship; it was like, "Well that's going to be me and that's what I want."'

It all began with a phone call bearing an offer from Macclesfield Town, who had the added attraction of being managed by Manchester United legend Paul Ince. It was the start of a professional career that yielded far from a king's ransom.

Reid began life as a professional footballer on £150 a week at Macclesfield in League Two. It went up to £350 after he had established himself in the team and by another £50 a week every season until his wage reached £650 a week by the time he left Macclesfield for Morecambe in 2011. Reid played 146 games for Macclesfield, scoring five goals.

At Morecambe, also in League Two, in his prime, he was on £1,000 a week, with win and goal bonuses taking it up to £1,200.

'And yet Joe Bloggs out there thinks you are big time!' he says with a chuckle.

Then came a gradual falling out of love with the professional game that he had yearned for all of his life.

'I remember sitting home one day, and reflecting, like it doesn't feel like it used to feel, it feels like, there is hidden agendas, there is a business, and there's lies, and politics, and I just thought it's messing with my happiness,' he says.

It was only a matter of time before Reid turned to semi-professional football that he could mix with a lucrative full-time job. He began training as an electrician at the age of 27 and qualified when he was 30.

'I know a lot of people turn their nose up at going full-time because of the simple fact there's more money doing part-time football, and doing a job. I know that's one factor, but for me, it's just the case of falling out of love with it really. I got to about 25, and just came a bit disillusioned, it really started feeling like a business, than like an enjoyable sport, because I mean like back in the day, I lived and breathed it.'

The tumble down the non-League ladder was far from comfortable. Hednesford, Telford United and Brackley Town.

'I'm asking for drinks, I'm asking for towels, and they're saying no, you have to bring that yourself, really? I suppose, that's just being naïve, not being a big-time Charlie is just like, no, they didn't give you pants or towels, and that was a shock to the system', and it was a headscratcher. Have I done the right thing here? So, yeah, a real eye-opener.'

Reid must have really loved football to have endured some of the pitches and places he played in the lower reaches of the football pyramid from Chasetown to Gresley Rovers where he made 33 appearances, with two goals, on one of the worst pitches in creation.

'The first day I went there; it was a Tuesday evening and a home game. I don't know if you've ever been to Gresley but it is one of the worst pitches I've ever seen, it's the only pitch I know that's got a hill one end, with a bowl in the middle, but then still on a slope, then it tilts off. It's a crazy pitch, I went off there on a Tuesday, walked to the changing rooms, the changing rooms are obviously horrible and old.'

In 2023, Reid was ready to let non-League football go. Until a call from the blue from an old team-mate coaching at Worcester City revived his interest. One of the points that helped swing the deal was that Claines Lane was only a six-minute drive from his home in Ombersley.

Reid spent half of his life putting up with good managers and strange managers who wanted to play him out of position and mess him about. He fought through a double hernia, a snapped Achilles tendon and a nasty ankle ligament injury, but is still battling father time.

'Tuesdays would roll around, and things like that and like, oh, training, because I just suppose it is just the norm when you're working and getting older, everything does become a lot more, wouldn't like to use the word a "chore", because I do enjoy it when I'm there, it's just the mindset of, "Oh my God, I can't down tools and watch TV and chill out, got to get ready now, got to go fuel myself, to go and train,"' he says wistfully.

Back to that WhatsApp message to manager Cornes calling on any players who wanted to leave, or strongly wanted to stay, to contact him to save time.

Reid said he wanted to stay.

'I would have been happy to end my career on a high in a championship season, but I still had the desire to play.'

In the middle of June, Cornes said yes.

'I think this is going to be my last season,' he says.

Didn't you say that last year?

'Yeah, I think I did!'

Our laughter echoes down the deserted streets of Ombersley to the green hills not too far away.

Chapter 26

From Worcester with Love:
A saviour for Stourbridge

WHEN NEIGHBOURS Stourbridge looked for a saviour to shake off the Southern League blues, the answer came from Worcester, with love.

You could argue that Stourbridge's young energetic manager, hired in June 2024, sprang from the womb of Worcester City.

A managerial move that also strengthened the historical bond between Worcester City, Stourbridge and Kidderminster Harriers, which has seen generations of players and managers switch between the three clubs for more than a century.

Liam McDonald sat there in front of a crowd of Stourbridge supporters in the social club at Amblecote on a Friday night with a microphone in hand and a reassuring smile. He brought with him a request for a 1,000-strong crowd for every league game; and a promise of promotion to the National League North. And for his third wish?

Patience for a three-year plan, he says.

McDonald didn't have to drive far to the unveiling. He may have been born in Solihull, in Birmingham, but has lived in Stourbridge for more than eight years. This undoubtedly endeared him to the home-grown owners of Stourbridge, who wanted a hands-on manager.

'We want him to get us up and keep us there,' says chairman Andy Pountney, who owns a freight business just down the road, on the microphone.

Around 50 fans sipped on pints of beer and cider, good news for the club. Stourbridge, like most non-League outfits, wouldn't survive without thirsty fans in the social club. The gathering would see the club move at least 150 pints.

The owners of the club must be throwing a considerable amount of money at this three-year dream. They won't say how much, but the whisper on the night is considerably more than last season in return for the Holy Grail of promotion.

With this cash, McDonald spent the summer bringing in virtually a new team from higher-ranked sides including his former National League North club Rushall Olympic; along with his former management team, who won't come cheap.

McDonald promises to dominate 80 per cent of games and 'try to win all of them'.

The fans breathe a sigh of relief.

He pledges to bring new technology to bear: GPS and Wyscout to track players' data and performance. Largely unheard of at Amblecote, where many people on the terraces don't even use GPS in their cars.

'Champions League stuff,' says the bloke sitting next to me as he takes another sip of Hobgoblin ale.

In this new era, Stourbridge will run out to play to the strains of an old home-grown song.

'It is by the Wonder ... what ? I am sorry, I am too young,' says McDonald on the mike to laughter from the floor and another warm smile from the new boss.

The song is by The Wonder Stuff – one of the few famous bands ever to emerge from Stourbridge.

On the cusp of their fame, in the early 1990s, I remember a couple of band members used to come to the odd Stourbridge game. Few knew who they were.

In fact, I didn't know The Wonder Stuff, whom I liked, were from Stourbridge until one of my journalist colleagues in London told me.

The song is the accordion-driven 'Welcome to the Cheap Seats'. It may backfire if Stourbridge struggle into a halfpenny place in the league next season. At the very least, it may help attract more supporters from the overpriced Premier League.

'Yeah, we want the fans to sing it when we win,' says McDonald. 'The players will sing it with the fans.'

The fans will be more than happy with just a few more wins, especially over teams which by rights shouldn't be on the same pitch.

All agree Stourbridge certainly need something. Eight years on from the giant-killing run to the third round of the FA Cup, it had been a miserable season for them. A handful of talented players, an armful of not so talented players, one or two past their peak, had seen the club end up rudderless and mid-table following a string of miserable defeats.

There were two swashbuckling wins of 4-2, one home, one away, over Kettering Town and Coalville in the first couple of games of the season, before a descent into frustrating mediocrity.

Even when they were winning, Stourbridge played with little belief, like they were two goals down.

The biggest problem for Stourbridge supporters – in the season where Worcester City beat all comers – was that their team made even more mediocre rivals like Bromsgrove Sporting and Halesowen Town look like Bayern Munich.

Ian Pilkington, like his father and grandfather before him, has been a long-suffering Stourbridge supporter all his life. He has been going to Amblecote since the early 1970s and followed the team away everywhere from Rothwell to Raunds; from Burton Albion to Buxton. An odyssey that took half a century and a ton of dedication to complete.

'I remember us being 3-0 up at half-time away at Buxton in the fourth qualifying round of the FA Cup in 2009. People on the terraces were still talking about the chances of Stourbridge throwing it away!' he says with a laugh.

Stourbridge won 4-0. It sent the club through to the first round of the FA Cup, for the first time in 133 years of playing football, where they lost 1-0 to Walsall at home.

In the early years of this century, Pilkington stepped into the breach to help run the club when they crashed out of the Southern League on the way to oblivion in 2000. He helped scrounge paint and volunteers to paint the ground. He dropped a few bob to a few plumbers he knew to fix the creaking pipes in the clubhouse.

For more than 20 years, he worked in the evenings on the Amblecote pitch to turn it into a green, smooth, carpet; tailor-made for passing football. It was labour which could have made a story in the Bible.

In the lean days, Pilkington became chairman of the club for a number of years while they tried to survive and find new investment. He stepped aside when Stourbridge-fan-made-good Pountney came in with new investment and a business-type approach. Arguably, without the latter, the club could have tumbled down the football pyramid.

In the last season, like many at Amblecote, he suffered more than his fair share of despair as he expected little and got even less.

'Shocking,' is a word that cropped up many times if you ran into Pilkington at the final whistle in the poor 2023/24 season.

'I think you just wish that things were better performance-wise. If they could get the right mix of people in. Improving some standards, we have a bit of fly-by-the-seat-of-your-pants attitude,' he says.

'Ball control should be better. We still have players who can't control a bag of spuds.

'We are in 2024, the club is stuck in 2010. The facilities are not great; you have a ground with three sides and an open side that nobody uses. It makes it difficult to manage,' he says.

Joe Billingham has been supporting Stourbridge for 60 years; he is one of the few fans alive who can remember them playing Wimbledon in the old Southern League in the 1970s. Like many Stourbridge fans he has lived and worked his whole life a free kick's distance from the ground. He is undoubtedly one of the characters of the Amblecote terraces who always stands behind the goal, in the same spot at either end, for almost every home game.

Every season he spends a fortune on petrol and hamburgers in following his club up and down the country. Every season he tries to visit a ground he has never been to, be it Leiston or Lowestoft. He has probably spent about five of the 60 years driving up and down the motorways of England as he rarely misses an away game.

At home games Joe's catchphrase is: 'Come on, Stour!'

Three words which the kids standing behind him on the terraces parrot back to him in satire.

Joe holds up his right index finger to salute the mimicry – which, after all, is the sincerest form of flattery – to a big cheer from the youths behind. Another joy of non-League football.

Bearing in mind Harold Wilson was in power when Joe started supporting Stourbridge, he probably has a right, more than most, to expect success on the green turf of Amblecote.

'Every July, all I want to see is one season, as I call it, in the promised land. We have been trying for 15 years to get out of this standard. I would just enjoy one season at a higher standard, just to see how well we could compete,' he says.

The man charged with bringing this about is McDonald, who has been handed a pile of cash and a ton of faith by the club's owners to bring Stourbridge back to glory. He is young for a manager in a career that's spanned nearly a quarter of a century and been busy, to say the least.

At the age of 39, he has managed three clubs and player-coached another, plus playing as a midfielder for at least eight clubs in a dozen years. He played for Tamworth before the TV cameras against Everton at Goodison Park in the FA Cup and has Tim Cahill's shirt to prove it.

McDonald's career took shape before big crowds and bright floodlights at Worcester City's St George's Lane. He admits his first club was the most influential in shaping his career. McDonald was in the first intake of Worcester City's short-lived Youth Training Scheme and the first to emerge from it into the first team, at the age of 18.

McDonald, born in Solihull, started his football career early. He left school at 16 and hunted for a club. He secured an apprenticeship at Rushden and Diamonds, but the hard-up club shut down the scheme before he had a chance to kick a ball in anger.

'Everyone wanted to go to a big club, but none of them made it. I was really keen to find a smaller club, but didn't have anywhere to go,' he recalls more than 20 years later.

'I knew Worcester was starting a football programme but didn't have enough players to fill the places. I went to a few trials and quickly realised I was one of the best players there. This was the start of my football journey.'

The deal was football training blended with study. The lads trained on the Claines Lane pitch – where the first team now play – for part of the week and studied at Barbourne College for the remainder.

McDonald studied for an NVQ in sports science and a National Diploma in applied science; qualifications that stand him in good stead in his current job as a head of year at a Birmingham school.

'It was a million miles away from the first team at this point. There were 20 of us from Birmingham, Worcester and Stourbridge. The Brum lads used to meet up with the Stourbridge lads at Stourbridge Junction railway station. There would be eight of us heading to Worcester, laughing all the way on the train.'

In the second year, McDonald captained the Worcester City academy side at a youth tournament. The team didn't win, to the deep disappointment of McDonald. It hurt so much he shied away from the prize presentation; not wanting to see the winners pick up their trophies.

'The coach Ray Woods, the head of the programme, told me to watch the presentation; obviously, he knew what was coming.

'The organiser said: "Player of the Tournament … Liam McDonald!"'

The prize was a brand-new pair of Adidas Predators.

'I was buzzing because back in the day, at college, I had mad finances and couldn't afford a pair of Predators. Back then, they were the boots to have.'

McDonald may have had the boots of his dreams, but he didn't yet have his league debut for Worcester City, something the ambitious teenager dreamt of more than anything.

By this time, John Barton – the man Worcester City sold to Everton for a record fee in 1978 – was the manager after a lengthy spell at Kidderminster Harriers. He saw something in McDonald and allowed the teenager to train with the first team.

'It was a fantastic education, training with legends. I was the butt of everybody's jokes being a small, spotty, young kid!!' he says.

'Among the players, John Snape took me under his wing as did senior players Carl Heeley, Paul Carty and Mark Owen. The manager John Barton was good to me.'

The break came on a cold January morning in 2004. Worcester City were playing away at Dover on 3 January, always a tricky game on the south coast against a tough little club.

McDonald sat alone on the coach contemplating the 400-mile, eight-hour round trip to Crabble, the home of Dover. He was going to be late home that night, without even kicking a ball.

All of a sudden, there was a flurry of activity on the bus as it readied to leave the car park at St George's Lane. McDonald watched Barton call his senior players to the front of the bus for an impromptu meeting. There seemed to be an issue.

The problem was first team regular midfielder Darren Middleton told Barton he had the flu and didn't feel well enough to play.

'All I heard was: "We've got to play him. Let's go and tell him to just play,"' recalls McDonald.

Five seconds later Barton and Snape strode down the bus and told McDonald he was in the team, in central midfield. He was 18 and on top of the world. That Saturday undoubtedly changed McDonald's life.

'That was it, I made my league debut, centre midfield, aged 18 years and weighing three stone. Just joking, but I was really skinny and very small. I was man of the match; the papers were, like, "amazing!"' he says.

Worcester City lost the game 2-1 to Dover. Owen scored their only goal, but McDonald won a break into the first team. He enjoyed a run of games as the season drew to a close, thanks to his dash in Dover.

'On the coach everyone was: 'Mac you were so good!' We lost but the Worcester fans didn't care. They were saying: "He is good and one of our own!"

'"We've got this player for free, plays in the first team and going to college." It was great at that moment, a lot of them, friends who went to league clubs and didn't make it had to come into non-League football in an attempt to earn a first team place. I was ahead of them.

'What I lacked in physicality, I made up for in fitness. I was really fit. Snapper [Snape] used to win the ball and give it to me. "I could do this," I thought,' says McDonald.

'It was just tremendous. I was enjoying myself for the first time, I felt I can really do this. I am left-footed, have got some tricks and I can run.'

Twenty years on former Worcester City manager Barton has no regrets about giving the young McDonald his debut at Dover.

'He had got something as a player. I would say he was creative, not everybody is blessed with his decent understanding of the game. You can't sit someone down and teach them understanding of the game,' says Barton.

'You could trust him. On the pitch, trust is a massive word. He was a good lad with a lot of discipline. The biggest compliment you could pay him was, whenever he was involved, he never let you down.'

Barton was one of the pioneers of the Youth Training Schemes, which spawned young talented players like McDonald.

The Worcester City Youth Training Scheme was the brainchild of Barton. In 1988, Barton was the head of the sports department at Burton and South Derbyshire College. He went to Sam Brassington, the chairman of Burton Albion, offering training schemes, which offered school leavers the chance to learn and play football at no cost to the club.

Brassington, who died in 2020 aged 79, dismissed the idea, saying it wouldn't work, according to Barton.

Early in the 1990s, undeterred, Barton went back to the Burton Albion manager Nigel Clough, who sanctioned it.

'I wish we had franchised it at the time, we would have made a fortune! We had an educational programme that was receiving government funding, so you could finance and run the programme properly,' says Barton.

Sadly, many of the well-meaning schemes, ahead of their time, were doomed, says Barton, because of old-fashioned greed.

'You have to remember a BTEC then was worth around £4,500 a year per head. We trained 18 lads in our first year. Because it was successful, people [colleges] started to get greedy and want 40 and 50 on it. You are dealing with somebody else's son. "I'm not doing 60," I told one college. They become mere income generators; morally it was wrong, very wrong. Today, there are some doing it well, plenty doing it not very well.'

McDonald played around 100 games for Worcester City before looking further afield for more first team football.

He didn't have to look that far; about ten miles down the road. McDonald headed for the bright lights of Bromsgrove Rovers, where his mentors Snape and Heeley were already playing and welcomed the midfielder with open arms.

A string of journeyman non-League clubs followed: Hednesford; Halesowen; Barwell; Kettering and Sutton Coldfield.

McDonald, a Newcastle United supporter who believes Alan Shearer was the best striker ever, always wanted a taste of the big time.

It didn't come until his time at the last club he played for: Tamworth, the pride of Staffordshire, then a National League team.

Tamworth fought their way through to the third round of the FA Cup in January 2012, nearly eight years to the day from when McDonald made his humble start with Worcester City at Dover. The club faced Everton away.

More than 5,000 Tamworth supporters travelled to Goodison Park in a blaze of blind hope and loyalty; such is the tradition among real non-League supporters.

'It was just walking out on to the pitch and the massive, massive stands towering above you. They probably had 15,000 in the ground just to watch us warm up. We came from playing for 1,000 people every week,' says McDonald.

In arguably better days, when the FA Cup was taken more seriously, Everton took to the game as if they were up against a fellow Premier League side.

United States international Tim Howard was in goal, England international Phil Neville was captain. Belgian international Marouane Fellaini roamed the midfield and Netherlands international John Heitinga scored the first goal, after only five minutes.

Leighton Baines, who played 30 times for England and 348 times for Everton, scored the second from the penalty spot. It was the cue for McDonald's entrance as substitute for the last ten minutes, the most memorable minutes of his career. I asked him about that feeling that many non-League players hold that they could, on their day, play just as well as the professionals.

'You do think, you could have done that. Until you get on the pitch with these players and realise that they are miles better than you! This was Everton at Goodison Park. You criticise these players on the pitch, then you realise how good they are!' he says.

'I got Tim Cahill's shirt. I remember standing in the players' car park after the game and seeing thousands of fans streaming past and some of them recognising you as someone who played in the game. It will stay with me as my greatest moment as a football player.'

McDonald needs a few more great moments as a manager if he is to revive the dozing giant that is Stourbridge. At his unveiling in the middle of June he was unequivocal.

'I want to get Stourbridge back to where it should be. We are going to have to start from scratch,' says new broom McDonald with another warm smile that would surely be wiped off his face in the event of going 3-0 down to Alvechurch, at Lye Meadow, on a wet Tuesday night. It can happen.

In this starting from scratch with a fresh team a few legends had to be scratched off the team sheet, including the player of the season: Charlie Price. The veteran goalkeeper suffered a season standing behind a porous defence and pulled off some of the finest reflex saves I have ever seen in non-League football.

In a move that could only happen in non-League football, Price disappeared down the road to rivals Bromsgrove Sporting. In the opposite direction came the much younger Ollie Taylor, a keeper that Stourbridge fans had been barracking for years!

Taylor is the son of former Fulham, Southampton and Birmingham City goalkeeper Maik Taylor. The father stands behind his son's goal at almost every game, throwing a few choice words of advice over the barrier. At the very least, McDonald will be assured of one regular supporter among the 1,000 he expects to flock to Amblecote for every game in the new season.

Joking apart, the fans are likely to flock back if McDonald can make like Chris Cornes, at his old club Worcester City, and deliver promotion and victory.

McDonald shows every sign of doing just that. He is an energetic, tracksuited manager with a good record in what he sees as a very rewarding, if difficult, job.

'It is very tough. You have a lot of commitment and your family has to understand the commitment, it is an opportunity to have a hobby to get paid. It is. It is more difficult to be a non-League manager. You are preparing from Monday to Sunday. It is a full-on job, but we enjoy it,' he says.

'You get to play football with a big smile on your face day-to-day. On the highs, I am on cloud nine. If we lose, I am rock bottom.'

McDonald entered management at a fairly tender age. You could argue he spun straw into gold, with a limited budget, at both Rushall Olympic and Solihull Moors.

The latter of the two clubs is now knocking on the door of the Football League. Rushall Olympic is a village team from Staffordshire which has managed, against the odds, to carve out a place in the National League North.

The new Stourbridge manager has come a long way, via Bromsgrove Rovers and Goodison Park, yet his humble start at Worcester City is rarely far from his mind as the club struggled against bankruptcy.

'I was sad to see everything that happened. I said to my lad, "I used to play for Worcester." It was a shame,' he says in the summer of 2024.'The positive thing is they are on the up again. Ryan Rowe and Cornes, a Worcester man, it was those two taking to the job that achieved promotion last season. Worcester can slowly get back to where they belong. It is a fantastic city with great fans, and they deserve better.'

It seems Worcester City will always be on his mind. 'I would love to manage Worcester one day. Solihull, Stourbridge but not yet Worcester!'

You wouldn't bet against it.

Chapter 27

120 Years in 12 Plastic Boxes

THE 122-YEAR history of Worcester City is safe.

All of these memories are kept for posterity in a garage in the small village of Bevere, just north of Worcester.

The story of Worcester City dwells in 12 plastic boxes, stuffed full of old programmes, photographs and newspaper cuttings, under the sharp and loving eye of volunteer club historian Julian Pugh the polite chronicler, par excellence.

We meet at a coffee house in the Shambles, just inside the boundary of the old city walls. It was called the Shambles because it was lined with butcher's shops, and like most streets in this ancient city it has a story to tell.

Pugh wrote in the programme for the final Worcester City game at St George's Lane, in 2013, how people used to run out of the shops on the Shambles to applaud Worcester City's first towering centre-half who played from 1902 to 1915.

Evesham-born Joe Gould signed from the defunct Berwick Rangers club and played 394 games for Worcester City, scoring five goals. He was a moustachioed giant, the heart and soul of the defence, who was described as a tough leader and club man.

With Gould leading the team, Worcester City won the Worcestershire Senior Cup six times in a row; in those days, a big deal.

You can only imagine the rapturous applause as he walked down the Shambles on his way back to his family home in nearby Charles Street, in Blockhouse.

When Gould, a brickyard labourer, retired in 1915, Worcester City couldn't stage a testimonial game for him because the First

World War was raging. The club gave him £20 for his service, worth around £2,600 today.

Just one of the hundreds of thousands of facts about Worcester City that live in Pugh's head and the 12 plastic boxes as he devotes a large part of his life to chronicling the club.

'I'm sure my wife despairs sometimes. But it is clearly what I enjoy doing. There is a part of me that says I need to pass all this on to someone, at some point. None of us are going to be around forever and somebody needs to inherit the responsibility, like I did,' says Pugh.

'There are a dozen plastic boxes full of things in my garage. They don't come into the house. I don't have a study or memorabilia room, or anything like that. But I do have scrapbooks from the 1960s.'

In the last 50 years, Worcester City may have tumbled to the bottom of the football pyramid, but in the field of keeping club records you could argue the club is in the Premier League.

Few clubs – especially in non-League – can boast an almost complete record of games stretching back more than a century, with a list of players, appearances and crowds.

This is the life's work of two men, Pugh and Brian Cook, who between them recorded every kick of the last 58 years, by 2023, with press cuttings, their own eyes and busy pens.

Cook, born and bred in the city, caught the Worcester City bug on the cusp of the FA Cup glory days of 1958, the season the club kicked Liverpool out of the competition.

He collected programmes and recorded results and signings from 1965. Cook snipped out more than 8,000 press cuttings, enough to derail a goods train.

These treasures were used as research for the *Official History of Worcester City FC*, published in 2003, the club's centenary year, written by Cook and Pugh. It is the supporters' bible and played a valuable part in the research for this book. It not only has goals and appearances, but also has dates, scorers and crowd figures dating back to 1903.

The modest and quietly spoken Pugh was also born and bred in Worcester. He went to Worcester Royal Grammar School, in the Tything, in the heart of the city, founded by the first Bishop of Worcester in 685. It is now a private school, but for centuries it took in the brightest young scholars in the city.

Former Pakistan Prime Minister and Worcestershire cricketer Imran Khan went there, as did Edward Leader Williams, the designer of the ground-breaking Manchester Ship Canal.

As a teenager, like many of us, Pugh found football was a way of getting out of the house on a Saturday afternoon. He became a regular at St George's Lane in the late 1970s when Worcester City laid waste to all before them.

'If I'm honest, Worcester used to beat every team. It is only when you watch football more that you realise most of it is disappointment, with occasional good times. It was entertaining football, Worcester won most games, scored plenty of goals. Of course I went with my schoolmates and it was the highlight of my Saturday,' he recalls.

'A couple of years later was the Southern League winning season under Nobby Clark and that is the season that everyone talks about – you can reel off the names: Jimmy Cumbes; Barry Williams; Malcolm Phelps; Kevin Tudor; Ralph Puncheon ... they are household names to Worcester City supporters.'

Pugh admits the path of true love for his club was rarely smooth.

'Then, as is the way, you discovered music, you discovered girls and going to the pub. I did try and keep the interest up for two or three years and then I decided I am going to make this the thing that I do on a Saturday and started to go regularly and stayed pretty much for 30, 40 years.'

Pugh loved the atmosphere at St George's Lane and always enjoyed the warmth of humanity around him, with all its flaws. On Saturday afternoons all of us youngsters enjoyed the theatre on and off the pitch. Pugh's face lights up as he tells his tale.

'What I realised, when you went to watch as a kid, grown-ups were let off the leash on a Saturday. Yes, you would smell booze and fags and cigars. On Boxing Day, there was the smell of cigars and whisky from hip flasks. The big thing is, you would hear grown-ups swearing – you didn't hear that in the street, or at home did you?' he smiles.

Not much, I agree, in those days when elders would admonish you with words like: 'I know your mother and father. I'm going to tell them what you've done.'

Between 1989 and 2003, Pugh was the programme editor, as well as working on his labour of love with Cook on *The Official History of Worcester City FC*.

So, when Cook knocked on his door at Bevere, bearing a pile of papers and cuttings, asking Pugh to take over as historian; the apprentice didn't have to be asked twice. At the time Cook had fallen ill. He died, aged 64, in 2009.

'He kind of said, right, here you are, it is your job to take this on from me now.

'It was bits of paper, CDs, a memory stick that sadly I can no longer access. It has an error on it, and I can no longer open it up again,' recalls Pugh.

'A lot of the stuff exists in other places. I am not an anorak. I always say to people, "I know some stuff, but I don't know everything and if you ask me a question, I could probably find out the answer." I won't churn facts and stats off the top of my head, a lot of people know stuff that I have forgotten and don't know and that is all part of learning and gaining extra knowledge.'

Pugh, who works for Worcester City Council in the Guildhall in the High Street, set to the job of chronicling the football club with a will. He found the internet to be a double-edged sword.

'The internet has changed things. Up to about the year 2000, you had to rely upon newspapers and books to get your information.

'Now stuff gets out there and you can pick it up on all sorts of sources, websites or Facebook or Instagram, or whatever. You need to verify information to find out if it is true. Wikipedia – as useful as it is – is not 100 per cent correct.'

Social media is great for sharing information, he says, but as we journalists know too well, it can lead to misinformation. Sifting it all in search of the truth is a lot of work, which Pugh does for love.

'If someone asked me how many games a player played, I don't have the information at my fingertips, I don't keep spreadsheets, but I can go and dip in and put it all together,' he says.

'Two things I do get asked to do is taking enquiries from people researching their family history and they know a little about their dad, who played football, and they know a little more about him. That is quite rewarding, if we can say we have a photograph of him in a team, or football kit and you can share it with a family ... Also, players pass away, sadly, and somebody has to write about their career for an obituary and that will always land in my lap.'

It is not always easy. The passage of 30 years can play tricks on the memory of a footballer.

'Occasionally you get disputes. Never want to fall out about it. What I have learned is that time plays tricks on the memory for me, just as it does to a footballer.

'Footballers have got their memories in their head, but they are not great on the facts and the stats. Sometimes, they will think that something has happened, which didn't happen, or they played in a game, which they weren't involved in. You don't want to destroy their kind of memories, you know?' he says.

'I wouldn't ever want to argue the toss and say, "No, you were on the substitutes' bench that day!" I can see a lot of affection for Worcester City; a lot of the players I come into contact with say they have really good memories of playing for Worcester, better than any of the other clubs they were with and I think that is credit to everybody involved with Worcester City over the years.'

In these difficult and humbling times for Worcester City, Pugh says it has been a pleasure to write a new set of records at the end of the storming 2023/24 campaign.

It was a record-breaking season which saw the highest points total of 101.

Worcester City also equalled the best-ever tally of games won in a season with 32 victories.

In the same season, the club also set the unbeaten away record of 18 wins and one draw.

There were 24 consecutive wins in all competitions.

A run of 31 games unbeaten, in all competitions, from 18 November to 13 April.

The fewest defeats in a season: five in all competitions.

Plus, the longest ever cup run, nine rounds in the FA Vase.

For a season which almost didn't kick off, amid bankruptcy and despair – these are memories worth holding on to for the fans and Pugh will see they are entered into the club's archive.

I wonder what was on the memory stick with the error? I am sure the industrious Mr Pugh will find out one day.

Chapter 28

The City Is Blue!

THERE WERE plenty of smiling faces and more than a few cans from Tesco Express on the platform at Worcester Foregate Street as the faithful gathered to journey to the last game of the season. At the end of a long and glorious campaign there were plenty of nods of recognition.

There was a feeling of celebration and spring in the air. Worcester City had won the league and all that was left was a journey to lord it over the country cousins of Pershore Town, just 20 minutes up the railway line from Worcester on a high-speed London-bound train, swifter than a Liam Lockett run down the left.

The weather wasn't playing ball though. Drizzle, yet again, accompanied by low black clouds. As we sped through the fruit valleys of the fertile Vale of Evesham, it looked a bit more like the Scottish Highlands in winter.

Pershore is a station that time seems to have forgotten. It lies in an industrial estate about an hour's walk from the town in the inevitable drizzle.

The good news was there were three generations among the families on the long walk to Pershore United. About 20 people on their way to the game more than two hours before kick-off – it could have made a TV advert for non-League football.

'How far is it, mum?' says a youngster in front of me. Flippin' far was the answer back from mum.

Pershore United is a quaint little ground, just behind the town's market. When I first saw it, I thought it was a school pitch, but there was no mistaking it as it filled up with hundreds of Worcester City fans. There was an air of expectation and excitement.

On the pitch, it was like shelling peas for Worcester City, the team was a slick act at the end of this season; 4-1 without even breaking sweat.

The most bizarre of the four goals was Kyle Belmonte's second. A Pershore defender tried to clear about 30 yards out and blasted the ball at Belmonte. The ball ballooned off Belmonte and went in over the head of Pershore's teenage keeper Josh Reed-Jones, who tried to back-track in vain.

What I like about non-League football is there was no jeering or mocking of the hapless keeper, just laughter along with the mishap, which could have happened to anyone.

At the end of the game the crowd surged on to the pitch to celebrate the presentation of the Hellenic League trophy.

'The city is blue,' they chanted.

Simon Lancaster, the owner of the club, was there just over nine months after he had rescued the club. Surely one of the last words on a fine season must go to him.

'I met two people at the game in Malvern, whom I'd never seen before and they said, "Are you Simon?" and they said, "I just want to thank you, this is the best football we've ever seen, brilliant, we're loving it." So honestly 98 per cent say they're absolutely loving it,' he says.

The club may have been successful on the pitch, but lost money again, which ultimately will come out of Lancaster's pocket.

'The trick is going to be to try and find a way to become sustainable, but of course, without our own ground, that becomes difficult, well that is difficult because three months ago, our earning potential was limited. So the golden egg really, was getting into our own ground, that's the hardest piece of the jigsaw to find, but yeah you know, we've still lost money, and predicted to lose money again this year.'

Lancaster is also looking at other clubs to see how he can raise income away from the pitch.

'The owner of Kidderminster, Richard Lane, who I know quite well, has offered to meet up for a coffee because he's quite into grants and what grants are available – a lot of obscure ones that you can't find online even, actually that you're entitled to, so he's going to give us a bit of a hand, bless him.'

Kidderminster also has a corporate hospitality scheme, I interject.

'Yes, and we're sort of replicating that. Some of our biggest clients have come off the back of that. They'll say, right, this construction company, they're a partner of ours, you're a partner of ours, we've got a dinner and a game on Saturday, we'll sit you next to them, sort of like the old-fashioned business networking.'

But it all hinges on planning permission for a new ground for Worcester City, which, at the end of 2024 still hadn't been applied for.

'I was with the Redditch owner a couple of weeks ago at our Worcester City goals day and he came to that, and they've got stuff going on seven nights a week at their place, they're hiring out the 3G, sportsmen's dinners, they're doing events, they've got the bar open seven nights a week, you know they've got kids playing football, parents in the clubhouse having a drink and it's just making money seven days a week, whereas we've only got Claines Lane for like two hours on a Saturday. Redditch also do really well with their events. They do a big event every couple of weeks really, so yeah, more events. The golf day was a success this year, that made us a good few grand. We can sort of expand things like that, so yeah, love to do more events outside of the matchday really. Like I said, our only revenue is Saturday afternoon really, so more events through the week and Friday nights and Sundays and stuff like that to be earning money more than one day a week really.'

Overall Lancaster is here to stay. He has been given a very gentle ride so far by Worcester City supporters; I haven't run into one in nine months, who dislikes him or what he is doing. I tell him this.

'Well, its's always OK when you are winning!'

We both laugh.

Epilogue

ON THE face of it, non-League football is in rude health in England. The game seems to have emerged strong from the paralysis of Covid to win back the crowds. Many non-League supporters have told me they wanted to go back to the grounds to feel human again.

There is no doubt that the standards of football, grounds and safety are much, much higher than they were even a decade ago.

The crowds appear to be coming back as fans get sick of VAR, the plastic Premier League and sky-high ticket prices in the top flight.

Maybe also non-League football is going through a renaissance as Brexit Britain searches for those touchstones of national identity. I can't think of anything as English as a quixotic tilt at windmills by a tiny football club in search of a bigger dream. It was heart-warming to see the renaissance of a great club like Worcester City through canny business minds and the sheer force of will by its supporters. I hope they do well and can win promotion again this season, but they must be ready for the drift away of supporters if the club starts to struggle.

What the research for this book has reinforced within me is the nobility of the millions across the nation who put down their hard-earned cash to watch non-League football despite knowing they will never get a Champions League spot – or win anything for that matter.

Then again, I think that is the charm of the game. It more resembles the lives of most people in the nation. It is closer to home and made by people who get up early in the morning and work like the rest of us. People who will shake your hand and pause for a chat whether you see them in the street, or are digging it up.

On the other hand, there are dangers looming. The cost of the game for a start; every year it goes up, with new safety requirements and rising wages.

If a club wants to progress it is going to cost more every season. Soon, won't there be complaints of ambitious non-League clubs pricing supporters out of the market?

A lot of the non-League supporters I saw in writing this book were fairly well-heeled pensioners enjoying 30-year, well-funded pensions. In this new age of contracts and zero-hour jobs will the pensioners have so much to splash on non-League football in 20 years' time even?

Then there's the youngsters. Will enough of them look up long enough from their iPhones to something out of a cold Tuesday night away game in the rain at Corby Town? Last but not least, non-League club owners and the authorities – by that I mean local government – need to sit down to work out what is the best plan to provide a sustainable ground fit for football, which will attract investors and grants from the Football Foundation.

Thirty years ago, you could play on a cabbage patch – as Wimbledon did – and make it into the English top flight. It didn't matter. Now you need a proper stadium.

Local authorities shouldn't hide from their responsibilities, as Dudley Council appears to be doing to the detriment of Southern League Stourbridge. They treat football as a builder of community and a developer of youth. For this to be so, the councils should be giving long leases and more support – after all, it's our money they are spending. They shouldn't just be there on the coach when the team makes the third round of the FA Cup to share in the glory.

That is the role non-League football has to play in our world and sense of identity. This can't just be a place where old men yearn for the past, but where young enterprising people plan for the future.

I am proud that I inherited the game from my father and grandfathers; prouder still that it has helped enrich my life. May non-League football not shrink from the challenges ahead and go from strength to strength.